Breaking Free
From Domestic Violence

JERRY BRINEGAR

HAZELDEN®

INFORMATION & EDUCATIONAL SERVICES

Hazelden
Center City, Minnesota 55012-0176
1-800-328-0094 (Toll Free U.S., Canada, and the Virgin Islands)
1-651-213-4000 Outside the U.S. and Canada)
1-651-257-1331 (24-Hour FAX)
http://www.hazelden.org

ISBN: 1-56838-288-X

HAZELDEN INFORMATION AND EDUCATIONAL SERVICES
is a division of the Hazelden Foundation, a not-for-profit organization. Since
1949, Hazelden has been a leader in promoting the dignity and treatment of people afflicted with the disease of chemical dependency.

The mission of the foundation is to improve the quality of life for individuals,
families, and communities by providing a national continuum of information, education, and recovery services that are widely accessible; to advance the field
through research and training; and to improve our quality and effectiveness
through continuous improvement and innovation.

Stemming from that, the mission of this division is to provide quality information and support to people wherever they may be in their personal journey—from
education and early intervention, through treatment and recovery, to personal and
spiritual growth.

Although our treatment programs do not necessarily use everything Hazelden
publishes, our bibliotherapeutic materials support our mission and the Twelve Step
philosophy upon which it is based. We encourage your comments and feedback.

The headquarters of the Hazelden Foundation are in Center City, Minnesota.
Additional treatment facilities are located in Chicago, Illinois; New York, New
York; Plymouth, Minnesota; St. Paul, Minnesota; and West Palm Beach, Florida.
At these sites, we provide a continuum of care for men and women of all ages.
Our Plymouth facility is designed specifically for youth and families.

For more information on Hazelden, please call **1-800-257-7800**. Or you may ac-
cess our World Wide Web site on the Internet at **http://www.hazelden.org**.

CONTENTS

Acknowledgments
Foreword
Preface

1 THE BREAKDOWN

2   THE ROOTS OF FAMILY VIOLENCE

3   STOPPING THE VIOLENCE

4 THE BREAKTHROUGH

ACKNOWLEDGMENTS

My commitment to stopping family violence is a "stand" for my children and all children. My kids are the first to receive my deep appreciation for their encouragement, support, and understanding. I often heard them say, "Daddy is at his computer again writing his book." Thanks, Keily, Autumn, and Kyffon—thanks for being you!

I also appreciate the helpful feedback, constructive criticism, contributions, and support of my colleagues: Don Cornelius, M.D., David Reed, Will Hart, John Dagley, Ph.D., Tim Evans, Ph.D., and Richard Endsley, Ph.D.

Most of all I want to express my gratitude for the patience and encouragement of my friend and wife, Meg, for hours of reading, proofreading, and being honest, loving, and tolerant . . . for believing in me and joining my stand for stopping domestic violence.

This book would not have been possible without the blood, sweat, and tears of my clients over the past fifteen years. Their struggles for survival and commitment to change have contributed greatly to this work. They have been great teachers and have courageously accomplished great recoveries. This book honors their work.

FOREWORD

Substance, readability, and clinical practicality characterize this book. Jerry Brinegar not only adds depth to our understanding of family violence, but he adds a compassionate and learned voice of realistic hope for victims, perpetrators, and obscure legions of helping professionals laboring together to make a positive difference in the destructive cycle of domestic violence.

The power of this book is in its encouraging message that we can do something about family violence. We don't have to just label it, condemn it, deplore it, or be incapacitated by our fear of it. Each of us involved with the family violence struggle—from within or alongside—can do something. It is this tone of encouragement built on substantive, practical strategies for action that makes this book a "must read."

The mastery of the book is its clinical wisdom. Brinegar writes with insight and conviction. He has built on the knowledge that he has accrued from years of real experience both as an ordained pastor and as a family therapist to provide concrete evidence that enough is known about family violence for effective action.

> —John C. Dagley, Ph.D.
> Associate Professor
> Counseling and Human Development Services
> University of Georgia

PREFACE

Juanita had been rushed to the hospital with her blood pressure sixty over twenty, with two black eyes, a broken jaw, several broken ribs, multiple contusions, and a dislocated shoulder. She was bleeding internally and near death. After seven weeks of intensive care, she was released on an outpatient basis. I met Juanita the day she was released. She sat in my office and told me her story.

> **My boyfriend and I went to a bar. There he took several Quaaludes and drank several beers. He became crazed, and I wanted to go home. In the car on the way home, he began punching me in the face and cursing me. I tried to get out of the car, but he sped so I couldn't get out.**
>
> **He drove me to his trailer and forced me inside. He kept hitting me and saying he was going to kill me. I began pleading with him not to do this, to leave me alone. He hit me so hard that it broke my jaw. When I fell to the floor, he began kicking me in the ribs and stomach.**
>
> **I managed to crawl to the bathroom and lock the door. In the mirror I saw that my face was twisted and bleeding.**
>
> **He broke the door down and dragged me to the bedroom and began beating me again while undoing his pants. I told him that I was dying, but he didn't stop. When his pants were around his feet, I ran past him and out the front door into the darkness. I flagged a car down—and that's the last thing I remember.**

Juanita lived to tell her story and to get help. At the beginning of her recovery, she was dependent on abusive relationships that involved alcohol and other drugs. With extremely low self-esteem, she was suicidal and had never stood up for herself. Even in telling this story about her near-death experience, she wavered on whether to help her boyfriend get out of prison by being a character witness at his early release hearing—and even wondered whether she should start seeing him again!

Fortunately, instead she decided to stay in therapy and follow the treatment plan that is outlined in chapter 3 of this book.

Several years later, Juanita was in full recovery from domestic violence. She met and married a healthy, nonviolent man and settled into a drug-free, abuse-free family. Happy, successful, empowered, and alive, Juanita had the courage to say no to any further abuse.

Millions of Americans, mostly female, do not say no to abusive relationships. They live in prisons of peril within their own homes. Beaten down, victimized, raped, and humiliated, they often don't know what to do or where to turn.

Every year in the United States, 2.3 million women are severely assaulted by their spouses; 1,300 are killed.

Children are primary victims, too, seeing the turmoil and living in fear of the next attack. Over six million children are severely assaulted by family members every year in the United States. Children learn to think that violence is caused by something they've done wrong, that they're to blame. They don't know where to turn or what to do. This book can help.

In *Breaking Free from Domestic Violence* is a special section of advice to victims of domestic violence. If you currently are being abused, you may want to turn directly to chapter 3, follow the instructions, and read the rest of the book later. It's important to get help now. Don't wait, like Juanita did, until it's almost too late. You may not be as fortunate.

Twenty years ago, anyone searching for information on family violence probably experienced frustration with the shortage of literature. Now we have facts, know many of the causes, and have made progress in raising public consciousness about the problem. Yet few books are available to help victims or victimizers.

Breaking Free from Domestic Violence briefly reviews the history and causes of family violence, examines several types of abuse, and—most important—gives substantial counsel on *what to do about it*. It is an invitation to heal the deep wounds caused by violence and abuse in your life. The healing will require three things from you:

1. learning more about what's happening to you;

2. making a commitment to getting the violence stopped; and

3. getting professional help.

The contents of this book represent a powerful course of study on domestic violence. Simply by beginning to read it, you are making a commitment to get the help you may need.

Whether you are being abused, doing the abusing, or both, you are not necessarily a bad person. You probably are repeating what you learned and have not developed alternatives for handling conflict and stress. The most important thing you can do is get help to stop the violence.

A word of caution: when entering into the process of healing, be prepared for disorientation on the way to a new orientation. Old ways of thinking were developed as survival skills and will need to be replaced.

For example, some parents would argue that hitting a child isn't so bad, that it is even necessary at times. This old internal monologue will not give way easily. Many victims of spouse abuse and perpetrators of family abuse become stuck. They don't know how to change or any reason to try.

A new internal message is: "It is wrong to hit any person." New monologues require a lot of practice. In solving problems of family violence, we have to practice new ways of thinking!

Insanity is doing the same thing over and over again and expecting different results.

Stopping family violence is going to require actions that will interrupt the repetitive videotapes and change the nature of thinking and being, of doing things differently. Recovery is demanding, but quite possible. It's up to you, and you can accomplish it!

To quote one adult survivor of family violence: "Be as committed to healing as you were to surviving your childhood."

I hope that this book will be an empowering experience to help you move your life from breakdown to breakthrough to a safer, healthier, and happier life.

1

THE BREAKDOWN

A father is irritable with his children, scolding them harshly as he put them to bed. The next morning he found a note pinned to his pillow that said, "Be good to your children and they will be good to you. Yours truly, God."

VICTIMS

Billy Edwards, sixteen years old and depressed, sat staring at the floor in my office. He was there to be "fixed." His parents had dropped him off for counseling to find out why he was thinking about suicide. He wasn't on drugs and couldn't give any specific reasons for feeling so down on himself. I asked him, "What was the ride over like?" He pulled further into himself. I repeated the question. Silence. I repeated the question again. Finally he began to talk.

His mother had punched him in the face in the parking lot. His stepfather had kicked him in the side for not cooperating.

The next session I asked his parents to come. When the subject of hitting came up, the stepfather readily admitted kicking Billy. "After all," he said, "he asked for it."

His mother denied abusing him. "I only hit him once," she said. Later she admitted to whipping him regularly. "It's not abusive. I don't use anything but a coat hanger."

These parents never saw the connection between their physical abuse of Billy and his suicidal depression.

Three wives, three children, and two husbands are killed every day by their family members.[1]

1

Family violence is an age-old problem. From the biblical account of Cain's jealous murder of his brother Abel to our daily news reports, history provides a continuing saga of family violence. This destructive pattern shatters families, which weakens the very fiber of our society. "Over six million children and three million spouses are severely assaulted each year."[2] "One in four girls and one in seven boys experience some form of sexual abuse before reaching age 18."[3] And at least half of these sexual assaults will be perpetrated by family members.

"Home Sweet Home"—I remember these cross-stitched words framed on the living room wall of our farmhouse in Missouri. It sent a message of hope to a family steeped in hard times. The home is supposed to be a sanctuary, a place of safety where children can play, explore, and learn. In contrast to this sentiment, the home has become one of the most dangerous environments in our society. "Women and children first" may be the chivalrous cry aboard a sinking ship, but unfortunately it applies to family violence as well.

Women: The Primary Victims

FBI statistics show that a woman is beaten in this country every fifteen seconds.

Historically, women have been oppressed and beaten with the approval of societies dominated by men. One ancient law decreed that a woman who was verbally abusive to her husband was to have her name engraved on a brick, which would then be used to knock out her teeth.[4] In the Roman Empire, a woman could be stoned to death if her husband accused her of not being a virgin on their wedding night. She had no recourse. Her husband also could divorce her by taking a piece of parchment and writing on it his declaration of divorce. Wife beating was expected when a woman "stepped out of line."

Rule of Thumb

The husband's right to chastise his wife with a whip or rattan no bigger than his thumb, a remnant of old English law, was upheld by a Mississippi court in 1828.[5]

In the United States, spouse abuse is of epidemic proportions. A 1978 study concluded that among the 47 million married couples in this

2

country, 2.3 million women were being physically abused and 1,300 women were killed by their spouses that year.[6] FBI statistics for 1984 indicate that 2,116 spouses were killed by their mates.[7] And a 1988 review of studies reveals estimates that spouse abuse occurs in 20 to 30 percent of all families.[8]

Sociologists Murray Straus, Richard Gelles, and Suzanne Steinmetz, in a 1980 ground-breaking national survey on family violence, found that one in four wives and one in three husbands thought that hitting one's spouse was a necessary and normal part of being married. Millions have laughed at Jackie Gleason ranting, "Alice, you're going to the moon!" while shaking an angry fist at his television wife in "The Honeymooners."

Fortunately, the feminist movement has confronted these attitudes, and spouse abuse is no longer considered acceptable behavior. Yet some men continue to abuse their wives simply out of fear of sharing empowerment with them.

No one deserves to be hit or battered. Women who find themselves victimized by an abusive relationship need to take immediate action. An abusing husband is just like a child, in that he will continue the behavior as long as it is tolerated and it works.

The first step is to admit that you're being abused and that you deserve to be treated with respect. It *is* possible to create a home environment that is safe and free from physical and emotional harm.

Children: Defenseless Targets

Like wife abuse, child abuse is as old as human history. Children, in the Hammurabi Code of 2100 B.C. and the Hebrew Code of 800 B.C., were considered property, and infanticide was an acceptable practice. In Roman times, the *Patria Potestae* permitted fathers to sell, sacrifice, mutilate, or kill their offspring. As documented by Suzanne Steinmetz in *Family Violence, Past, Present, Future*, "The practice of burying children in the foundations of buildings existed throughout history, and as recently as the sixteenth century, German children were buried alive beneath the steps of public buildings."[9]

In 1986, 2.1 million cases of child abuse and neglect were reported in the United States, according to statistics from the National Committee for the Prevention of Child Abuse. Of those investigated, 737,000 (or about 42 percent) were confirmed, meeting specific criteria. Fortunately, a case does not need to be confirmed before the family is offered preventive services. A large number of cases cannot be confirmed because the family disappears. Less than 2 percent of reported cases are estimated to stem from false allegations.[10]

In 1990, 2.5 million cases of child abuse and neglect were reported. This represents an increase of 4 percent in the past year, 31 percent in the last five years, and 117 percent in the past decade.[11] Children between the ages of three months and three years are the most vulnerable.

In America in 1646, a law attempted to help parents control their rebellious children. It stated that "unless the parents have been very unchristianly negligent in the education of such children or have so provoked them by extreme and cruel correction, any child over sixteen years of age and of sufficient understanding who cursed, smited and would not obey his natural mother or father, then would be put to death."[12]

A landmark in the shifting of public consciousness came in 1874. Mary Ellen, a nine-year-old, was defined by social workers as a member of the animal kingdom so she could be protected under the law designed to protect animals from cruelty, since there were no such laws to protect children. "Public reaction to the need to sue the Society for the Prevention of Cruelty to Animals to protect children was instrumental in the founding of the Society for Prevention of Cruelty to Children."[13]

In 1984, a six-year-old boy appeared on "Good Morning, America." He had been set on fire by his father! Ninety percent of his body had been burned, yet somehow he survived. His father is serving thirteen years in prison for this sick crime. The little boy's eyes were captivating: sad, hurt eyes in a totally deformed, disfigured face. The program was directed at wakening America to the problem of child abuse. Bumper stickers saying *IT'S OK TO TELL* became the craze. Like most fads, the bumper stickers have nearly disappeared and the problem is still with us.

Edwin S. is a decorated Vietnam veteran who has spent the last twenty years drifting and drinking, disturbed by nightmares about someone trying to kill him. He has become a recluse, trusting no one. He has been unable to hold down a job longer than three months at a time—either he's fired or he quits in anger. He has been through three marriages, all involving spouse abuse and substance abuse.

Vietnam post-traumatic stress disorder? Yes, but it goes farther back than that. The dysfunction in Edwin's life did not begin when he was a machine-gunner in Vietnam. It began when his father savagely and repeatedly beat him as a young child. His father hit him with his fists, boards, a razor strap, and fencing wire. His mother also beat him.

When Edwin was ten, his mother divorced and remarried. His stepfather actually tried to kill him with his bare hands. Edwin spent the night with blackened eyes and a broken rib cage, shivering under a bed. The next morning, his stepfather found him and resumed beating him. Edwin escaped and ran away. For the next several years, he lived where he could, terrified of a hostile adult world. He found a home in the marine corps but soon found himself terrified again in the hostile environment of the Vietnam jungle.

Abused children may never be able to trust and love other people; without help, they may always have an attitude of inferiority and alienation.

A child needs a sense of security to become a socially productive citizen. Children need to know that family rules are designed for order and functional living. In his book *Power and Innocence: A Search for the Sources of Violence*, Rollo May talks about this matter by describing what he calls nutrient and integrative power.[14] Nutrient power is a power *for* the other person and is best illustrated by the functional parent's caregiving to his or her children. Integrative power is a power *with* the other person. It is a level of harmony and accommodation in a given relationship.

Children need parents who are *for* them and *with* them in life. Abused children miss out on nutrient and integrative power and often grow up to be dysfunctional, antisocial individuals, retaliating against anybody who gets in their way. Alfred Adler found that when people are treated in a "less than" way of being, the payback is inevitable.

"Gun just went off," says daughter of mom's death.

Rashunda Golden, seventeen years old, as reported in the *Atlanta Journal/Constitution* on December 10, 1987, testified that her mother had beaten her severely and that she had been sexually molested by her mother's boyfriend for almost ten years. Rashunda was on trial for shooting her mother in the forehead as she (her mother) was beating her half-sister, Melinda.

The payback isn't always this severe, but sooner or later abused children retaliate, sometimes at innocent bystanders. Often the payback is equal to the violence they experienced. It also shows up in other forms of antisocial behavior, such as stealing, vandalism, and robbery.

We must stop family violence to protect not only its victims, but also our social order and community safety, which are being threatened as well. The state of the family reflects the state of society. If we want a better and safer community, we must stop family violence.

Elise Boulding, a noted sociologist, says that we need to consider the family's role in untangling our social confusion. The home is where people first learn to live with one another, where they learn to love, hate, get angry, fear, forgive. The home needs to teach how to love and work with others, how to handle emotions, and how to forgive. With these lessons mastered, our children will be able to develop their full potential.

Every day in the United States, 100,000 students in public schools are carrying guns!—"The Today Show," January 12, 1990

The family is the place where one's world is formed. I do not believe that life has any higher priority than parenting and providing a safe, functional environment for our children. The best effort is given in teamwork between mother and father, although single-parenting efforts can be preferable to being raised by parents in a dysfunctional marriage.

Whether from a single-parent home or one in which both parents are present, children need guidance and security from both genders. Henry Ward Beecher once said, "What the Mother sings to the cradle goes all the way down to the coffin."

Augustus Y. Napier asserts, "What kids rarely get is an involved, strong, nurturing father who is there for them. If our society could change this system, if we could insert an involved, committed father into the everyday lives of his children, if he could become a figure of emotional support directly to his wife, we could change the course of human history."[15]

What the mother sings to the cradle too often includes tolerance of abuse and abuse itself. Instead of a strong, nurturing, involved father, the child gets an angry, depressed father who sees nothing wrong with using physical punishment. After all, *his* parents acted the same way. The child who is hit, sooner or later hits back, either physically or by other methods—power struggles, behavioral problems at home and at school, hitting or bullying other children, withdrawing into isolation, running away, promiscuous behavior, alcohol and other drug abuse, and even suicide. We get what we give.

Our children can be seen as mirrors. If we yell, they yell; if we hit, they hit; if we swear, they swear; if we abuse alcohol or other drugs, they'll probably do the same.

Elders: Often-Forgotten Victims

"In December of 1984, my son attacked me with a hatchet while in a drunken rage. I struggled with him, but he was able to strike me in the hip with the hatchet. Fortunately, the physical injury which I suffered has healed with time. The emotional and mental scars do not heal so easily. I am a victim of elderly abuse by a family member," reported an elder in a prepared statement before the Subcommittee on Health and Long-Term Care, House Select Committee on Aging, May 10, 1985.

Every year in the United States, 1.5 million
elderly people are abused by their older adult
children or caretakers in their family.[16]

Elderly people are the chronological opposite of children but similar in dynamics—defenseless, vulnerable, and available. Who would think of harming a hair on Grandma's head or pushing around Grandpa? It's almost unthinkable, but then so is every other form of family violence. It is estimated that four out of five cases go unreported due to fear, coercion, embarrassment, or inability stemming from physical or mental impairment. If this is true, as many as five to six million cases of elder abuse may be occurring each year in this country.

In 1988, the House Select Committee on Aging estimated that one in every twenty adults over the age of sixty-five is being mentally or physically abused. This violence is escalating. In 1980, one million cases of elder abuse were reported; by 1988 that number had increased to one and one-half million cases reported.[17]

Our elders are being "beaten, denied food, forced to remain in their rooms, tied to their beds, raped, tricked or forced into handing over their money."[18] The typical victim is a woman, seventy-five years or older and dependent on caretaking. While all fifty states have laws that require reporting child abuse, thirteen states have not passed reporting provisions for abused elders. Public interest wasn't aroused until the late 1970s and even then was received with mixed feelings. We are taught to respect and honor our elders. It's inconceivable that we could harm them.

Many of our nursing homes are understaffed and overfilled. Even under the best of circumstances, our grandparents are often given over to the care of someone else with a sigh of relief. Given adequate legislative support and funding, nursing homes and retirement centers can provide safe, efficient care when it is necessary. Care for the elderly can be a privilege of dignity and honor in the home as well as in a caregiving institution.

Earlier I mentioned how important it is for children to feel secure and safe in their environment. Imagine yourself in old age, knowing that you can't live much longer. Ask yourself this question: "Can I take care of myself as well as I did when I was young?" The answer is obvious. G. Jay Westbrook, a gerontologist in California, says that "age makes the elderly more vulnerable than they've been at any other time in their lives." The elderly need protection and help just like children and other victims of family violence.

Siblings: Accepted Violence

When I was growing up, the Brackson brothers next door had a reputation for being tough. Their toughness was learned at home. One day they came tumbling out of their house into the yard already bloodied. They both grabbed short two-by-fours from under their porch and began beating each other. Only death or exhaustion could have stopped that battle. Fortunately, it was the latter.

No one reported the Brackson boys. After all, they were brothers! Sibling violence has been virtually ignored in our society, accepted as normal rivalry. Murray Straus found that sibling violence exceeds the level of violence that parents use on children or that spouses use on each other. He traced more than 36 million attacks in 1980 that would have been considered assault had they not occurred between siblings: in a single year, 5.8 million siblings beaten up; 14.5 million hit with an object; 15.2 million kicked, bitten, or punched; 290,400 threatened with a gun or a knife; and 109,000 attacked with a gun or a knife.[19]

Sibling violence must be condemned! It is problematic because it is learned behavior modeled after parental and community behavior. Like incest, it knows no boundaries and contributes to the breakdown of society in crime and violence. If siblings are not taught to honor and respect one another, it's doubtful that they will honor and respect neighbors and friends. Boundaries of behavior are crucial to the survival of community living.

Student Abuse: Is Your Child Safe?

In 1982, third-grader Teresa Garcia of Penasco, New Mexico, refused to be paddled for disruptive behavior in class. Her teacher, J. D. Sanchez, held her upside down while the school principal, Theresa Miera, struck her legs with a paddle.[20]

On a spring day in 1987, Jamie Logan, a sophomore at Portsmouth West High School in Scioto County, Ohio, left the school lunchroom to call her orthodontist after her braces had started to dig painfully into her gums. Because she had not asked permission to leave, Jamie was given a choice by the assistant principal, Paul Meeker: detention or a paddling. Jamie relied on the school bus to get home, so she chose the paddling. According to Jamie's father, James Logan, Meeker gave Jamie "two massive licks: the first sent her against the wall, bruising her chest. The second made it impossible for her to sit."[21]

In May 1987, Ruby Cunningham of Jacksonville, Texas, asked her five-year-old daughter, Crystal, how she had gotten the bruises on her bottom. Crystal told her that she and a classmate had been paddled twice by Mary Sue Bruno, the principal of Westside Kindergarten School, and three times by her kindergarten teacher, Rosa Cook. When her mother asked why she had been paddled, Crystal said, "I guess it was for playing."

The next day, Mrs. Cunningham took her daughter to school and demanded an explanation from the principal. According to Mrs. Cunningham, the principal explained that she had told a group of children, including Crystal, to stop giggling in the hall. When the girls persisted, the principal spanked them.

Six-year-old Ashley Johnson was one of the other children who had been paddled for the same offense. Her grandmother discovered Ashley's black-and-blue bottom, notified authorities, and took her to the hospital emergency room. Doctors told her that her granddaughter had been a victim of child abuse. Since the paddling incident, Ashley has had nightmares and has often awakened screaming. In a lawsuit filed in the U.S. District Court in Tyler, Texas, a grand jury found against the plaintiffs on the grounds that corporal punishment is not unconstitutional under the Eighth Amendment.[22]

According to a U.S. Department of Education survey, more than a million students were spanked in public schools during the 1985·86 school year.

Dr. Marilyn Gootman, an assistant professor of early childhood education at the University of Georgia, tells the story of a child who was paddled so severely by his teacher that he was taken to the hospital. The hospital notified authorities to report a case of suspected child abuse. The authorities left when they found out that a teacher, not a parent, had inflicted the child's wounds. Gootman asks, "Is it right to allow teachers to commit an act that could land a parent in jail?"

Why include corporal punishment in the school systems in a book on family violence? The school system is an extension of the family. During the school year, teachers actually spend as many or more contact hours with children as do the parents. From age five through adolescence—our children's formative years for personality development—they are shaped by their environment. The educational system is a significant part of that environment. Violence in the school is as traumatic and detrimental to the child's well-being as is violence in the home.

Violence produces violent results! We know that children who are hit in school often hit other students and lash back at teachers. We know that truancy, property damage, and antisocial behaviors are linked to being abused. Dr. Gootman raises an interesting parallel between corporal punishment and sexual abuse. She writes, "The use of the paddle becomes even more sinister when we try to draw the line between physical abuse and sexual abuse...and realize that the line is thin."

"If children are to understand that nobody can violate their bodies, they need to be protected not only from sexual abuse, but also from corporal punishment, because the two can readily be confused," says Sol Gordon, Ph.D., a sex educator and former director of the Institute for Family Research and Education at Syracuse University in New York.

Preventing the sexual abuse of children begins with stressing to them that they have the right to guard the privacy and integrity of their bodies.

Paddling often requires children to expose private body parts. According to Gootman, we cannot afford to be ambiguous about this matter. "Young children need to know that their bodies should never be violated, by anyone!"

Sexual abuse in the school system is unthinkable, but it is a very real problem. In 1984, for example, Raymond J. Cullen, then dean of students at Madison High School in Madison, New Jersey, pleaded guilty to misconduct and criminal sexual contact in connection with spanking a seventeen-year-old male student.[23]

A sixteen-year-old boy is encouraged to write a critical report on the high school administration and is promised that it is confidential. The paper is so good, however, that the teacher shows it to the principal. The next day, in class, a red-faced principal opens the door, loudly calls the young man out, and then literally pulls him to the front door of the school by the ear, saying, "If you don't like the way I run this school, you can leave."

Just as family violence took years to be recognized as a social problem, abuse in our educational system is still selectively tolerated. Children who are punished physically by teachers and principals learn that violence is acceptable and are likely to imitate violent behavior. Most of the nation's 12,000 school districts have abolished corporal punishment, but state legislation lags behind; only twenty-two states have put the policy into law.

They are Alaska, California, Connecticut, Hawaii, Iowa, Kentucky, Maine, Massachusetts, Michigan, Minnesota, Montana, Nebraska, New Hampshire, New Jersey, New York, North Dakota, Oregon, Rhode Island, South Dakota, Vermont, Virginia, and Wisconsin.

Diagram 1

The ten states with the highest percentage of children paddled every year:

Arkansas	13.70%
Alabama	10.31
Mississippi	10.30
Tennessee	8.76
Oklahoma	7.81

Georgia	7.81
Texas	7.79
Florida	7.05
South Carolina	5.56
Louisiana	4.92
United States average	2.67

The ten states with the most students paddled per year:

Texas	260,386
Florida	111,194
Georgia	93,006
Alabama	77,949
Tennessee	65,308
Arkansas	64,444
Mississippi	55,673
Oklahoma	51,306
Ohio	43,426
Louisiana	38,730 [24]

TYPES OF FAMILY VIOLENCE

What is family violence? Abuse occurs in five categories:

1. Physical abuse

2. Sexual abuse

3. Psychological or emotional abuse

4. Destruction of property or pets

5. Sociocultural abuse

Physical Abuse

Physical abuse is any physical action toward another person: pushing, hitting, whipping, biting, holding down, throwing, slapping, and spanking. Physical violence can produce bruises, concussions, welts, broken bones, and broken lives. When a person is hit in any way by another human being, it is demeaning. When people are hit, they also receive a message of worthlessness. The victim may think, "I'm no good; therefore, I deserve to be hit." The emotional damage from being abused creates a tremendous burden on the person's ability to cope with life.

Many abused persons turn to physical violence, leading to failed marriages and broken homes, alcohol and other substance abuse, homicide, crime, and even suicide.

> **Ninety percent of criminals in the United States reported being abused as children.**[25]

Sexual Abuse

Sexual abuse may occur between a married couple as marital rape. Any sexual abuse toward other family members is considered incest. Incest is the ultimate teaching that there are no boundaries, no responsible limits within which to live a normal, healthy sexual life. Incest victims often become promiscuous in their adolescence or later in life, or they retreat completely into the privacy of the family secret at home. A child commonly become obese to avoid being used as an object of gratification by a sexually abusive parent. Though most reported incest cases involve father-daughter relationships, occasionally both parents participate in the sexual violence.

Marianne J. is an example of biparental abuse. She had been sexually abused by her father at the age of ten and as an adult had worked through many of her trust issues and deep-seated fears of men. But she kept presenting an even deeper fear of women. She didn't understand why she resisted establishing close, intimate relationships with women. In one session, while in a hypnotic relaxation exercise, she was asked to go back, in memory, to the most painful experience with her father. She did this readily enough, but then she began feeling a lot of discomfort.

"There's someone else on the couch holding me down while he's doing it to me."

"Who is it?" I asked. "Can you see this person?"

She struggled to identify this person. After a few moments, she began screaming and crying, "It's my mother; it's my mother!"

Soon after this revelation, Marianne began to see that she had enabled an incestuous relationship between her husband and her daughter from her first marriage.

Confused boundaries and unstable personalities often result from sexual violence.

Adult victims of child sexual abuse may discover that sexually they have become addicted to clandestine relationships. "He pulled his hand out of my pants and spit on his fingers and rubbed them together. He didn't even seem aware of me. The sound of his spitting made me sick. Then he put his hand back down my pants and started to say something in that singing voice he used. The front screen door slammed and his hand ripped out of my pants like it was burned. Then he turned on me and whispered harshly, 'Don't you say anything to your mother ever. If you do, you'll be sorrier than you've ever been in your life.'"[26]

Threatened with harm by the perpetrator if she or he "tells," the victim is obsessed with keeping the family secret. This obsession with secrecy becomes a driving force in the individual's sexual development. Sex in clandestine, forbidden, fearful ways is learned. Multiple affairs can become the "drug" of the abused. Guilt, a familiar feeling associated with sexual abuse, sets in and lasts until the next cycle of desire and search begins. It's a vicious circle, as difficult to break as alcohol and other drug abuse. The high peak of excitement, danger, and stimulation keeps the habit intact. The adult survivor asks, "Is this the only way to be loved?"

One can even become driven to attract attention in provocative behaviors that have "little girl" or "little boy" characteristics. This attention-seeking behavior has much to do with low self-esteem and insecurity. Children are not ready for adult sexuality!

When abused by an adult member of the family, children become stage-level entangled. This means, for example, that a twelve-year-old is likely to express her sexuality throughout her adult life at a twelve-year-old level of development, with confused boundaries. Intimacy is constantly sought and rarely attained. Shame, humiliation, and dishonor weigh heavily on the victim's psyche.

Of the reported cases of child abuse and neglect, 15 percent involve sexual abuse.[27] A study of violent prisoners in 1986 reported more than 40,000 young victims—71 percent of them had been raped or sexually assaulted.[28]

Psychological or Emotional Abuse

The boundaries of psychological or emotional abuse often are difficult to define. Emotional abuse is far more than the usual form of cursing, blaming, threatening, and manipulating. It includes humiliation and deprivation, conversations that tear down self-esteem.

Spouse abuse does not always end with divorce. It may shift from physical abuse to psychological warfare. The scars from psychological damage go as deep as physical wounds and actually may take longer to heal—if they ever do heal. Therapists' offices are filled with adult survivors of child abuse and spouse abuse working through bad memories and the accompanying deep wounds.

Child neglect leads to emotional abuse, too. Of the reported cases of child abuse and neglect, 46 percent involve neglect, with an additional 9 percent classified as emotional maltreatment.[29]

Withholding affection and kindness can be crippling to children, marriages, and family relationships. I remember a children's sermon during a church service where the minister talked about how "arms are for hugging." At the end of his brief homily, he asked the children to hug one another. Two visiting children, a brother and sister, stood motionless and did not participate. They appeared to be quite uncomfortable. I knew they had a history of being emotionally abused and had never learned how to use their "arms for hugging." These children were simply "not doing" what their parents were "not doing."

Verbal abuse can become a prison. Raymond M. was always told by his father and brother in angry tirades and chiding rebukes that he was nothing but a "dumb kid" who didn't know anything and couldn't do anything right. As a young man, it seemed that Raymond had not been able to do anything right. Everything he touched seemed to fail. His teachers, in a typical Pygmalion effect,* discouraged him from thinking he was college material; so he joined the navy.

Once out of his original environment, he began to get different

---

*Pygmalion effect: the student fulfills the preconceived expectations of the teacher—for example, the teacher's pet accomplishes high grades because of the teacher's estimation of his high IQ. The student may or may not have a high IQ.

Not every psychologically abused child escapes so easily. Most children who are given negative messages about themselves grow up believing them and act out those self-defeating messages.

messages. The navy suggested he join their Polaris submarine program because of his high achievement level on entrance recruit exams. He began to change the way he thought about himself and took a few correspondence courses while in the service. His tutors gave him positive feedback and encouraged him to attend college.

Raymond applied for college entrance upon discharge. When his application was accepted, he had to decide whether he was truly a "dumb kid" or whether to believe the navy, his correspondence tutors, and the college registrar. He decided to enter college. By his sophomore year, he received a scholarship, and two years later, he graduated with honors. Several years later, when he decided to work on his doctoral degree, his brother said to him, "What do you want to do that for? We won't be able to talk to you anymore!"

Destruction of Property or Pets

Dan R.'s divorce led to angry, unresolved battles that culminated in his finding his entire collection of model airplanes, a lifelong hobby, piled on the living room floor in splinters. Alongside the pile was his expensive customized guitar, a mess of twisted wire and splintered wood.

Violence against family members often is expressed in the destruction of their favorite property. Examples from my family therapy practice include: hosing down a baseball card collection, smashing china, punching holes in the wall, taking a sledge hammer to car windows, ripping clothing, burning stamp collections, and breaking records and tapes.

Violence against a victim's pets is even more cruel. A man once sat in my office and told the story of how, as a child, he was served his pet rabbit for dinner. He had begged his father not to kill it. He had raised "Nibbler" as a pet and then was forced to eat him. With every bite, his hatred for his father deepened.

Violence against property and pets usually represents a prelude to physical violence. Victims should take every precaution to avoid escalation of the violence.

Sociocultural Abuse

Several years ago, a popular book shocked the public. *Sybil* was the story of a young girl who was severely abused by a schizophrenic mother. The little girl escaped her mother's torturous cruelty by devel-

16

oping multiple personalities. As often happens in sexual abuse, the child mentally dissociated and left the scene.

Her mother wasn't Sybil's only abuser. The town doctor and nurses, her minister, the neighbors, and her father all knew about the abuse, and yet no one did anything about it. In alcoholic families, this maintenance of the family secret—alcoholism—is called enabling. In the case of family violence, it is social abuse. Family, friends, neighbors, and community professionals have a responsibility to intercede in family violence. *It really is okay to tell*.

Many remember the classic story of the young woman in New York City who was accosted and repeatedly stabbed by a man while neighbors watched. Kitty Genovese was returning to her apartment in Queens when attacked. Neighbors heard her screams for help and watched the assault from their windows, but no one called the police. Sociologist Richard Gelles says that the neighbors' apathy did not reflect a lack of concern or a wish not to get involved. He concluded that "many of the witnesses thought that they were seeing a man beat his wife, and that, after all, is a family matter."

Sociocultural abuse is very complex in that it extends to the environment and the world community.

WAKING UP TO THE PROBLEM

Dr. Suzanne K. Steinmetz, a noted authority on family violence, notes four stages in the process of a society's recognition that a type of behavior or social phenomenon is a "social problem."[30] The **first stage** involves selective inattention, when the behavior is largely accepted as the norm.

The **second stage** is public awareness as the result of media coverage of the growing consequences of the behavior. We did not take seriously the problem of family violence until the late 1960s, when a paper on the "battered child syndrome" by Henry Kempe and his colleagues caught national attention. Within a few years, all fifty states had enacted legislation mandating the reporting of child abuse.

The **third stage** is "characterized by the onset of systematic research." In 1974 Congress created the National Center on Child Abuse and Neglect, which was authorized to study the problem and develop programs for treatment and prevention.

The **fourth stage** is action oriented. This is the stage we have now reached. The 1980s produced a national campaign slogan, "It's

OK to tell," followed by increases in cases being reported. With widespread public concern, more shelters for battered spouses, and protective custody for children, reports of child and spouse abuse began to decrease toward the end of the decade. The task before us in the 1990s is to continue our commitment to stopping family violence (see diagram 1).

A **final stage**, "the elimination of domestic violence," is not seen by Steinmetz as very realistic, given how our society values privacy and independence. We precariously walk the tightrope of when to get involved and when not to. We may need to raise our social consciousness so that those being studied, researched, and treated are empowered as well.

In the following chapters, you will learn some contributing factors of family violence and how to stop it. I invite you to take a stand with me to stop domestic violence in this decade, to make a safer environment for each other, our elders, our children, and our grandchildren. It's going to take a concerted effort. The beginning is in recognizing that we have a problem, educating ourselves about the causes of the problem, and then doing something about it.

**I stand for stopping family violence
in this decade.**

NOTES

1. M. A. Straus, "2001: Preparing Families for the Future," National Council on Family Relations Presidential Report, January 1990, p. 26.

2. Straus, p. 26.

3. Georgia Council on Child Abuse, brochure, 1990.

4. S. K. Steinmetz, *Family Violence, Past, Present, Future* (Newark: University of Delaware, 1971), p. 726.

5. Ibid.

6. J. P. Martin, ed., *Violence and the Family* (New York: John Wiley and Sons, 1978).

7. D. Finkelhor, G. T. Hotaling, and K. Yllo, *Stopping Family Violence: Research Priorities* (Beverly Hills, Calif.: Sage Publications, 1988), p. 24.

8. E. Stark and A. Flitcraft, "Violence among Intimates: An Epidemiological Review," in *Handbook of Family Violence* (New York: Plenum, 1988), pp. 293-317.

9. Steinmetz, p. 728.

10. National Research Center, 1986 Caseload Data (An association for protecting children; A division of the American Humane Association).

11. National Committee for the Prevention of Child Abuse, *Current Trends in Child Abuse Reporting and Fatalities: The Results of the 1990 Annual Fifty State Survey*, April 1991.

12. Steinmetz, p. 728.

13. Ibid.

14. R. May, *Power and Innocence* (New York: W. W. Norton, 1972), p. 109.

15. Augustus Y. Napier, "Heroism, Men and Marriage," *Journal of Marriage and Family Therapy*, January, 1991, vol. 17, p. 9.

16. Rosalie F. Wolf, Ph.D., "Testimony on Behalf of the National Committee for the Prevention of Elder Abuse before the U.S. House Select Committee on Aging, Subcommittee on Human Services," *Journal of Elder Abuse and Neglect*, 1990, vol. 2.

17. Ibid.

18. M. J. Perry, "Problem Gains Attention," *In Focus: Elder Abuse*, November 1985, p. 4.

19. Steinmetz, pp. 737-38.

20. Marilyn Gootman, Ed.D., "The Teacher Hit Me, Mommy," *Redbook*, October 1988, p. 131.

21. Ibid.

22. Ibid.

23. Ibid.

24. Georgians for Positive School Discipline, College Park, Ga., p. 3.

25. Georgia Council on Child Abuse, brochure, 1990.

26. E. Bass and L. Davis, *The Courage to Heal* (New York: Harper and Row, 1988), p. 19.

27. National Committee for the Prevention of Child Abuse, *Current Trends in Child Abuse Reporting and Fatalities: The Results of the 1990 Annual Fifty State Survey*, April 1991.

28. U.S. Department of Justice, Bureau of Justice Statistics, Violent Crime in the United States, no. NCJ-127855, March 1991.

29. National Committee for the Prevention of Child Abuse, *Current Trends in Child Abuse Reporting and Fatalities*.

30. Steinmetz, pp. 737-38

2

THE ROOTS OF FAMILY VIOLENCE

Many abusive parents share a childhood secret: they, too, were victims of abuse.

MAN CHARGED IN SUFFOCATION
OF THREE-YEAR-OLD

Baton Rouge, LA—A man was held in the death of a three-year-old who apparently suffocated when she was force-fed an entire chocolate cake, police said. Frank F. Johnson, 46, was booked Sunday on a murder charge, accused of failing to help Myra Griffin when the incident occurred Dec. 21.

Myra's mother, Marjorie Griffin, 23, of Baton Rouge was charged with first-degree murder last month. She is accused of force-feeding the child. "This was a cake she had made for the child, and she was determined the child was going to eat the entire cake," Officer Jeff Wesley said. "When the child refused to eat the entire cake, she force-fed it to the child. Allegedly." An autopsy found Myra suffocated because her stomach and throat were stuffed with so much chocolate cake that it blocked her windpipe, Deputy Coroner Chuck Smith said.
　　—*Atlanta Journal/Constitution,* January 16, 1990

Why does this kind of unthinkable violence occur? Tracing the roots of family violence requires an eclectic approach. One of the most commonly agreed on causes of family violence is that it is learned.

HISTORY OF FAMILY VIOLENCE

Violence is a learned pattern of behavior that has its roots in early childhood experiences. A child who sees his own mother beaten by his father is likely to grow up to abuse his wife. Likewise, the abused spouse is more apt to have had a violent father than a nonviolent father. We are creatures of habit. If violent behavior was the everyday experience while growing up, it becomes the pattern of our adult relationships. We repeat the role models of our parents.

Parents who were abused by their parents are six times more likely to abuse their own children.[1]

Violence in the family serves as a training environment for children. A child does not have the cognitive abilities to know what is right or wrong in parental behaviors. If the father uses a belt, it must be okay. If the mother slaps the child in the face, it must be okay. If the father and mother cuss, scream, and hit each other, that must be how boys and girls treat each other.

A study of thirty-three adolescents who had committed murder found that they shared a similar childhood background of relentless brutality, personal experience with violent death, and extremely unfavorable home conditions. Also, "a brutalizing childhood was found to be characteristic of rapists as well."[2]

Willie B. was notorious for his rage. Fueled by a drinking problem, he would relentlessly attack his children with verbal assaults, leather straps, and belts. When his teenage daughter would "get out of line," he would grab her long hair and drag her through the house. His children lived under the threat of abuse. In conversations, he avowed how important it is to break children's spirit to make them behave. He compared disciplining his children to training a dog. "You have to let them know who's the boss! Otherwise, they'll run all over you."

Where did he learn this way of thinking and being? As a young child, he was whipped and beaten constantly by his parents. When he was twelve, his father beat him severely and was holding a concrete block over Willie's head when a visiting matriarch intervened. Willie's mother, during an argument, threw a kitchen knife at him and missed. Willie's childhood was one of learning that violence is a way of expressing emotions and handling conflict.

But what about his father? Where did he learn the violence? When Willie's father was young, he was regularly and severely beaten by *his* father. When he became a strong teenager, he engaged regularly in fistfights with his father—usually to stop his father from beating and kicking his mother.

In the above case history, it is easy to see the cyclical nature of family violence. A partial genogram—a map of family history—is shown in diagram 2. This pattern of learned abuse exemplifies the Intergenerational Transmission of Personality Predisposition. In the early years of life, children's personalities are formed. An early experience of anger and violence predisposes their personalities to being angry and abusive. As we shall see later in this chapter, abused children are abusive to other children, animals, and their environment.

Sociopsychological predisposition is based on the child's parents and home environment (see diagram 3). If a girl's parents were depressed, it is likely that she will learn depression. If the mother or father had low self-esteem and their conversations keyed on negativism or pessimism, the child may model her own self-esteem and thought processes after the parent(s). If a parent is sexually abusive or displays infidelity, the child may pattern his or her own sexual behavior with boundary confusion and abusive behavior.

Parents do not awaken in the morning and consciously think, "Today I will abuse our children." Parents end up abusing their children for many reasons. Emotionally immature parents seldom understand their child's behavior and stages of development. One couple whom I counseled reported spanking their eleven-month-old child for continuing to cry after they told him to stop. Eleven-month-old children do not understand a command to stop crying! They cry for specific reasons. It is their communication to the world that they need something— to be fed, changed, held, or protected.

Another reason that parents abuse their children is lack of parenting skills and education. They don't know how to raise a child. Many abusive parents are repeating the model they experienced as children. Poor self-image, stress, alcohol and other drug problems, and social isolation contribute to child abuse. A parent with low self-esteem often will expect his or her child to meet emotional needs and will react abusively when disappointed. A child who feels the responsibility to meet his mother's needs in a bad marriage can be over-whelmed and then abused when he fails to measure up to the "missing dad."

Diagram 2

THE CYCLE OF FAMILY VIOLENCE

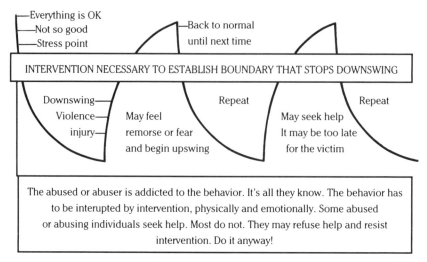

*See Chapter Three for more information on intervention

Social isolation can be a breeding ground for violence. A family that is living near other relatives and neighbors is more open to observation and intervention, whereas an isolated family is less influenced by social standards.

Sociocultural predisposition includes the child's geographic environment. A city or town with a high crime rate teaches fear and distrust. It also can influence a child's experimentation with breaking social rules. If the consequences of antisocial behaviors are not taught, children don't learn accountability for their actions.

Diagram 3

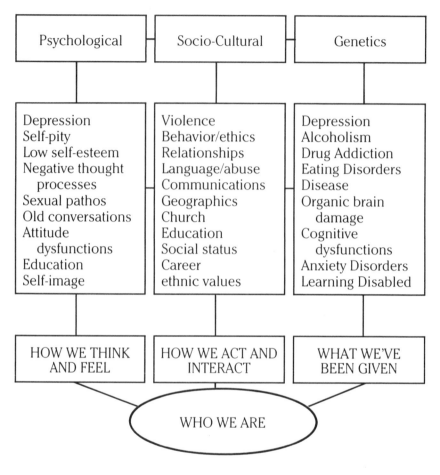

Psychological	Socio-Cultural	Genetics

Depression
Self-pity
Low self-esteem
Negative thought
   processes
Sexual pathos
Old conversations
Attitude
   dysfunctions
Education
Self-image
	Violence
	Behavior/ethics
	Relationships
	Language/abuse
	Communications
	Geographics
	Church
	Education
	Social status
	Career
	ethnic values
		Depression
		Alcoholism
		Drug Addiction
		Eating Disorders
		Disease
		Organic brain
		   damage
		Cognitive
		   dysfunctions
		Anxiety Disorders
		Learning Disabled

HOW WE THINK AND FEEL	HOW WE ACT AND INTERACT	WHAT WE'VE BEEN GIVEN

WHO WE ARE

INTERGENERATIONAL TRANSMISSION
OF PREDISPOSITION

Sociocultural predisposition also includes a child's educational experiences, friendships, peer pressures, church teachings, and politics. These factors can be very positive. I remember, as a boy growing up in a small midwestern town, how influential the local pool hall owner was among young boys. Gilbert Anderson was an esteemed father figure and mentor about life, as well as someone who taught a sharp game of snooker. Often he would use the game as a teaching aid.

"Life is like this game of snooker," he would say. "You have to know where you're aiming and where it's going to leave you. Sometimes you have to make your shots softly and other times with firmness. Always try to avoid being snookered!"

One of his favorite sayings was "Never say die!" Gilbert, on the sociocultural level of predisposition, was a very positive contribution. He and his wife, Annie, were community parent figures who taught recreation with responsibility and the consequences of misbehavior.

Genetic predisposition is important in predicting violence. Depression, alcohol and other drug abuse, anxiety disorders, cognitive dysfunctions, and learning and behavioral disorders all may contribute to family violence. Our inherited tendencies, however, are a complex interaction of the psychological, sociocultural, and genetic categories of predisposition.

An old Hebrew tradition illustrates this cycle of family violence in the statement, "The sins of the father are given unto the seventh generation." The original Greek translation of the word *sin* means "missing the mark." Family violence certainly misses the mark! It has no social value. Remember, 90 percent of all criminals reported that they were abused as children.

Today we know that the pattern can be changed and the abused individual can break free of domestic violence.

ALCOHOL AND OTHER DRUG ABUSE

**Alcohol and other drug abuse precipitates violence
in 50 percent or more of all domestic abuse.**

Individuals who use alcohol and drugs are more prone to violence than those who don't. A parent can be like two different people, with and without the effects of alcohol and drugs. Sober, the parent is gentle and kind; intoxicated, he may become aggressively punitive and cruel. Substance abuse escalates a person's loss of control and diminishes the ability to think rationally.

Alcoholics frequently display characteristics of irresponsibility and inability to tolerate frustration. They may deny responsibility for their actions and usually are married to a spouse who has sufficient personality disturbances that support—and even encourage—their mate's drinking problems. An addictive relationship is a permanent mate-to-mate relationship or a parent-child relationship that can be broken only if either person becomes a whole person who accepts full responsibility for herself or himself.

A client of mine described the dependent relationship she maintained with her husband even while living in separate houses. The path between their homes on the same property was seldom used except when her husband was out of liquor and on a binge. She would go to the store, purchase whiskey, and deliver it to him. She thought she was helping! When I suggested that she stop buying and delivering for him, she protested, "How will he get his liquor?"

When she became aware of how she needed him to be drunk in order to feel good about herself, the path became overgrown with weeds. She left the unhealthy relationship to get on with her life.

It's hard to break out of an addictive relationship. Codependents frequently display their own compulsive behaviors, such as anorexia nervosa or bulimic eating disorders. They can be as addicted as their partners to what Martin Heidegger coined "a state of forgetfulness of being": as long as I'm locked into the addiction, it frees me from dealing with the reality that is current in my life, such as a bad marriage, sexual problems, low self-esteem, financial difficulties, and so on. And as long as I can keep our relationship focused on my partner's addiction, the heat's off my problems.

In "We're a Nation of Addicts," Ann Wilson Schaef lists seven paradigms of addiction: self-centeredness, the illusion of control, dishonesty, confusion, denial, perfectionism, and forgetfulness.[3] These seven characteristics are equally true of the addict's spouse and children.

Though alcohol and other drug abuse may not be the cause of violence, supporting evidence suggests a positive correlation. In one year of my clinical practice at New Beginnings Marriage and Family Therapy, at least 95 percent of all adult children of alcoholics reported being abused physically and emotionally as children, and 75 percent reported some form of abusing their spouse or children.[4]

The current label "adult children of alcoholics" is viewed by some professional therapists as a counseling fad. I hope that it will become a permanent diagnostic category in the diagnostic manual for mental health practitioners, the American Psychiatric Association's *Diagnostic and Statistical Manual of Mental Disorders*, third edition, revised (*DSM-III-R*). It is a classification with substance and aptly describes the symptoms of confusion and problematic behavior that are associated with growing up in an alcoholic family.

If you suffered from the effects of being raised in an alcoholic home, reading Janet Woititz's book *Adult Children of Alcoholics* may seem haunting. She writes as though she had been an invisible guest in your home, writing down the action as it happened and the resulting scars and damaging memories. It's as though she had followed you around, taking notes on life in the shadows of a raging father and enabling mother, towering larger than life, creating fear where security was needed, distance instead of closeness, rejection instead of acceptance, punishment instead of discipline, anger instead of laughter or nervous laughter instead of safe joy.

Woititz knows about curling up in a fetal position under the bed, hiding, staying out of the way of uncontrolled fury, hoping that your shivering and shaking would go unnoticed. She knows about burying your head under the pillows to muffle the yelling, cursing, and screaming. She understands wondering on special holidays if it was going to be family day or a day of hell to be survived. She's seen marriages falling apart, with individuals consumed by fury and unable to love. Woititz is not a transcendental psychic. Anyone raised in a home where alcohol or other drugs were abused could have been taking the same notes, reporting the same experiences.

Adult children of alcoholics grow up in dysfunctional families. The degree of dysfunction depends on the combination of other contributing factors mentioned in this chapter. Dr. Woititz lists thirteen perceptions of the typical adult child of an alcoholic:

1. Adult children of alcoholics guess at what normal behavior is.

2. They have difficulty following a project through from beginning to end.

3. They lie when it would be just as easy to tell the truth.

4. They judge themselves without mercy.

5. They have difficulty having fun.

6. They take themselves very seriously.

7. They have difficulty with intimate relationships.

8. They overreact to changes over which they have no control.

9. They constantly seek approval and affirmation.

10. They usually feel that they are different from other people.

11. They are super-responsible or super-irresponsible.

12. They are extremely loyal, even in the face of evidence that the loyalty is undeserved.

13. They are impulsive. They tend to lock themselves into a course of action without giving serious consideration to alternative behaviors or possible consequences.[5]

LIFE CYCLE STAGES

Violence is most likely to occur in young, immature relationships. Seventeen-year-olds are hardly prepared for marriage, let alone child-rearing. When a teenage or very young mother or father has a baby, the baby's natural immaturity will be in conflict with the parents' youthful immaturity and lack of parenting education.

One mother in her twenties sat in my office describing her frustration and inability to get her ten-month-old baby to stop crying. She said, "I change its diapers; I get it a bottle of milk; I hold it . . . and it still cries! I even spank it, and that makes it worse."

Notice the use of "it" in reference to her child. The baby is an object to her, a foreign object that interferes with her life and untrained expectations about parenting.

Another parent, a twenty-three-year-old father, reported, "Sure, I play with my son. But when he gets too rough or won't stop playing when I tell him to stop, I whack him up the side of his head. He gets the message for a few seconds. Then he's right back doing what I told him not to do. So I whack him again, only harder. It's frustrating, because then he starts screaming and hollering. That's when I really lose it!" His son is five years old.

Any mature parent who is familiar with a child's stages of development will know that five-year-olds do not stop playing when told to do so. They're at a stage of developing their own sense of power and control of their life—testing limits, testing boundaries. They're not going to stop doing what they're doing simply because you want them to. They respond to distraction and affection. Hitting them teaches that they have no power to determine what they do. They're likely to withdraw and develop low self-esteem.

Children are not objects to be controlled. They are people with equal rights. They are our future. We design the future as we design our children. We would do well, therefore, to have more positive influence on young parents.

THE NATURE OF VIOLENCE

Sigmund Freud believed that violence and aggression are instinctual, inescapable facts of human existence. Violence is innate—that is, it is inherent in the genes of the species. Some convincing studies support this particular theory. Konrad Lorenz agrees with Freud and adds that violence has played a role in the survival of the species, which ensures that the genes of the stronger male and female will be passed on, a "survival of the fittest."

Lorenz notes that "animals have built-in inhibitions that prevent their aggression from resulting in death."[6] For example, wolves will fight only until one acknowledges defeat with an act of vulnerability that signifies surrender. The victor, having an opportunity to kill the defeated wolf, shows mercy and turns away. The fight is over. Such inhibition doesn't seem to exist among humans. Man is the most violent animal on earth.

Erich Fromm has stated that violence is learned behavior. One explanation for the human race being more violent is our higher level of brain capacity, which has created technological weapons that far surpass the "teeth and claws" of four-legged creatures.

Lorenz says that "the existence of weapons makes killing easier for human beings."[7] It is much easier to pull a trigger than to destroy another human being with your own two hands.

Erich Fromm notes that animals will attack only if there is an actual physical threat to their well-being. For humanity, Fromm adds "psychological threat" to "actual" physical threat. He adds that violent behavior is learned from one's environment.[8]

In an experiment conducted by Albert Bandura, a group of children between the ages of three and six were allowed to observe an adult teacher battering and abusing a large inflatable doll. When left alone with the doll, these children literally "beat" the doll. Another group of children, the same ages, also were allowed to observe an adult being gentle and nonviolent with the doll. When left alone with the doll, these children were gentle and playful. Inferences can be drawn on the impact of TV violence on both children and adults.

TELEVISION VIOLENCE AND VIOLENT TOYS

Our national diet of cruel, violent entertainment increases the danger of violence in our personal lives, communities, and international relations. Only Hong Kong and Mexico equal the United States in TV violence. According to the 1982 surgeon general's expert task force, the evidence is now "overwhelming" that violent entertainment has a harmful effect on people and on society as a whole.[9]

In a study of adult attitudes and TV viewing, George Gerbner of the University of Pennsylvania found that as the number of TV viewing hours increased for middle-class adults, their support for military expenditures increased. Other attitudinal changes linked to heavy TV viewing were what Gerbner calls a "mean world syndrome": fear of walking in the neighborhood at night, handgun ownership, ownership of large watchdogs, opposition to freedom of speech for people with different opinions.[10]

Thomas Radecki, M.D., has been an expert witness in eight murder trials involving violent entertainment. He tells of one case where a fourteen-year-old boy in Orlando, Florida, had started playing war and learning martial arts at age ten. The boy gradually escalated—along with his friends—from toy guns, to BB guns, to real guns. He even persuaded his father to buy him an AR-15 semiautomatic rifle, which he skillfully converted into a fully functional M-16.

He immersed himself in war films, and was constantly fantasizing about violent maneuvers. He and his friends would play war with real guns in the parks of Orlando. They pretended to patrol and would fix people in their gun sights. Fortunately, they would simply declare people dead without pulling the trigger.

The group needed funding for one of its war fantasies, based on the Hollywood war film, *Red Dawn*. The young men planned a trip to Colorado to set up their base camp for defense against a Communist invasion. They decided to rob a convenience store. The robbery began smoothly, with careful military planning, but things did not go as expected. The fourteen-year-old, dressed in full battle gear, was stationed outside the store. When a clerk resisted, the boy ran inside, shot him, jumped over the counter, and stabbed him in the throat.

Dr. Radecki reports, "When I examined the boy in county jail, he was reading Vietnam War novels from the prison library. He admitted that during much of his waking life he fantasized about military activity. He saw himself as simply a 'good, clean-cut American'; his dream was to be a U.S. Army Ranger, or a mercenary helping the Nicaraguan contras. He did not understand how he and his group could actually have killed someone."[11]

With TV's three major networks averaging 9.5 violent acts per hour on prime time (NBC is highest, with 10.6, and CBS is lowest, with 8.4) the problem of violence in our society needs citizens protesting and lobbying for healthier programs that provide mature, nonviolent role models for our children.[12] The average child will view 250 war cartoon episodes and 800 war toy ads this year on TV, the equivalent of 22 days of classroom instruction in violent behavior.[13]

Bob Dart of the *Atlanta Journal/Constitution*'s Washington bureau reports that children's programs—mostly cartoons—contain nearly five times more violent acts than do prime-time shows.[14]

According to an article in the *Atlanta Journal/Constitution* (January 26, 1990), 90 percent of the programs during children's hours (mostly cartoons) are violent.

NCTV News reports that "the rate of violence for weekend daytime children's programs was 18.6 violent acts an hour before 1980 and 26.4 violent acts an hour after 1980."[15] And according to the Nielsen Index, "American children see an average of 18,000 television murders before graduating from high school."[16]

POWER

Violence and aggression are only symptoms of what's wrong with our society and not the disease. The real disease is powerlessness.
—Rollo May, Ph.D.

Rollo May teaches that violence has its breeding ground in impotence and apathy and that a "state of powerlessness" is the source of violence. "As we make people powerless, we promote their violence rather than its control."[17] The word *power* comes from the Latin *posse*, meaning "to be able." Everyone wants "to be able."

In family violence, May states that "violence is most apt to occur between persons who are closely tied emotionally and, therefore, vulnerable to each other." The most dangerous room, he says, is the bedroom. It is the most murderous room in the house and is where most marital homicides occur. Married couples who establish a relationship in a "less than" condescension, traditionally with the male in the superior position, are creating the ingredients for violence.

Parents can and must learn from this theory about powerlessness as it relates to their children. I have counseled many children because of their violent outbursts and hostile statements. In 90 percent of these cases, the child has been abused, either physically or emotionally, or both. A child who feels powerless will set up power struggles with powerful behaviors. Children are almost always expressing their anger about being treated in a "less than" manner by a parent.

According to Dr. May, power has five levels: exploitive, manipulative, competitive, nutrient, and integrative. These levels are described in the following pages.

Exploitive power is the most destructive. It is violence in its rawest form. Exploitive power assumes violence as a solution and victims as nonpersons. It is a power of force that destroys human lives indiscriminately. If a person's power develops to this level, he is "out of control." Hitler and Manuel Noriega are two examples of men who used exploitive power. Men who hold exploitive power "obliterate" an enemy so as not to have any further problems.

Fortunately, the majority of parents and spouses do not practice this type of power. However, as you have seen in the case examples and news releases throughout this book, it is a significant problem in our society.

Manipulative power is destructive, too. It is power over another person. Violence is used when considered necessary. Manipulative power uses people as pawns in a political or personal "game of chess." "Con artists" are a good example of manipulative power. They do anything necessary to get what they want. They can be very dangerous when their schemes are resisted or confronted.

Manipulative power can be detected in the behavior of abused children. In cases of incest, for example, a child is manipulated for the adult's pleasure. In turn, the child grows up learning to manipulate others, sexually and otherwise. Seduction becomes a weapon instead of a healthy, mutually agreed upon experience. Sex becomes a means to get what is wanted, whether it's money, closeness, or power. A physically beaten child may grow up using physical threats and violence to get his way.

The middle level of power is **competitive power**. This is a power against the other person or people. In its most destructive form, competitive power destroys a community, a company, a relationship. It can pit one person's or nation's value system against another in an either-or situation.

Some people believe that competition has no beneficial social value. It can be very detrimental to a child's self-esteem to be compared to an older or younger sibling's talents or attributes. Each child needs to learn that he or she is "enough" without comparison. Our educational system, as well as the home, is a major contributor to competitive power.

Our very social structure is based on competitive power. In its most creative form, competitive power brings out the person's or company's or nation's best efforts, and everyone abides by the rules of "fair play." It is hard to imagine our society hiring on a first-come basis. And as long as we consumers have a choice of products, we will choose according to competitive priorities. As a society, we need to find balance between our teaching children to strive for their best and our nurturing their developing self-esteem.

Nutrient power is power for the other person. This is a community-building power that provides mutual respect and recognition without competition. Everyone is valued as a significant part of the total community. Nutrient power is a power that our helping professionals, as well as community citizens, would do well to adopt. Power is shared with equity. Everyone has the opportunity to contribute and be a part of the action. Nutrient power is a goal for parental power and child power, a standing-for each other.

I know how important it is for my son to know that he is loved and accepted just the way he is, and we have a wonderful ritual of nutrient power. Every night before bed, I tell him that he is my favorite little boy in the whole world and that I am fortunate to have him as my son. His six-year-old response is just as empowering, "You're my favorite daddy in the whole wide world. I love you too, Daddy!" Nutrient power is like a healthy meal of balanced nutrition.

The most creative form of power is **integrative power**. This power is not only *for* other persons but *with* them as well. It combines the strength of nutrient power and steps into a level of intimacy that places each person with—as well as for—the other. The power of a healthy parent is both nutrient and integrative. I am not only for my children, I am with them.

I grew up learning that Russians were all Communists and were to be identified as the enemy. This led to an "I'd rather be dead than Red" mentality, a learned listening. When I was forty-five, I traveled to the Soviet Union to see for myself these dreaded people who lived on the brink of invading my sacred homeland. The first shock to my learned listening was on the flight from Frankfurt, West Germany, to Moscow when I couldn't tell who was Russian, German, or American (except by language).

My experience in the Soviet Union was amazing! The majority of the people were not Communists, and they were some of the friendliest people I have ever met. Another shock was finding out how intensely they live in fear of Americans! One *babushka* (grandmother) came up to me, bowed her head, and with tearful eyes, said, "Please, don't bomb us!"

I sat by the Gulf of Finland as the sun was setting over Leningrad, thinking of how American missiles were aimed at me and Russian missiles were aimed at my family, who were seeing the same sun rise as I watched it set. At that moment, I realized the empowerment of integrative power as a possibility for stopping violence all over the world, as well as in the home. To do so will take a significant overhaul of the way we think and more education to counteract existing prejudices.

The Georgians in southern Russia have an interesting ancient custom. A Georgian family exchanges its youngest child with a family of another nation, to be raised in that land. They believe that as long as each country is raising a child from the other country, they will never go to war with each other! It's something to think about. Pay attention to how different you are with a friend's visiting child. You treat that child the way you want your own child treated when he or she is in your friend's home.

In summary, the use of exploitive, manipulative, and competitive power can produce violence in relationships. Nutrient and integrative power produce healthy, nonviolent relationships.

STRESS

Stress is an overworked topic these days, but it is a very real problem in family violence. It has many sources and is related to everything already mentioned. Stress is a precipitating trigger of family violence.

A specific situation of stress is seen in the bad marriage. Carl Whitaker, M.D., an experiential psychotherapist, says that a "bad marriage produces hateful demons out of perfectly nice people."

When Mom and Dad are in severe conflict or breakdown, the family is in severe conflict or breakdown. Children who grow up in bad-marriage homes have a dysfunctional model of what a family can be.

Worse, often the child is directly abused as the victim of the bad marriage. David Rothenberg will never forget!

CALIFORNIA BOY STILL FEARS FATHER, WHO SET HIM ABLAZE IN '83

David Rothenberg will never forgive his father for setting him on fire, saying [that] Wednesday's release of the man who disfigured him leaves him terrified despite unprecedented measures to keep the felon away. Rothenberg, Sr., set fire to his six-year-old son in a Buena Park motel room in 1983 after a telephone argument in which his estranged wife said Rothenberg would not be able to see David again. "If I can't have him, nobody else can," Rothenberg said when arrested six days later. Wearing a lapel pin reading, "Kids are the nicest people," he told arresting officers he was going to kill himself but was too much of a coward. Little David, dragged from the inferno by motel guests, suffered third-degree burns over ninety percent of his body.[18]

This extreme example of violence resulted from someone in a bad marriage who also was unstable and psychotic, fortunately a rare combination.

Children are the innocent victims in bad marriages. The best gift a parent can give his or her children is to constantly work on the marriage and provide a stable model of intimacy.

If parents divorce, then the best gift they can give their children is to put aside their own self-interests and work together for shared parenting. (Joint custody is not an answer when abuse, especially child abuse, is involved.) Divorce wounds children. The depth of the wound will depend directly on the parents' level of maturity and mental health. With professional help that prioritizes the care of the children involved, parents can minimize the traumatic effects of divorce.

Children are impressionable. They learn from their parents and other adults in their lives. If they see optimism, they'll learn to be optimistic; if they see pessimism, they'll be pessimistic. The following example illustrates how influential these learned attitudes can be.

Michael Popkin, Ph.D., author of *Active Parenting*, tells a story about two children.

> One of the children was outgoing and happy, and always saw the bright side of life. The other, introverted and sad, always saw the negative. . . .
>
> A psychologist proposed an experiment to see how far the differences between the children went. He put the pessimistic, sad child in a room filled with dozens of exciting toys. The other child, optimistic and happy, was put in a room knee-deep in horse dung. After thirty minutes the psychologist went into the first room and found the little pessimist crying amidst his toys.
>
> "But I wanted a scooter and there aren't any!"
>
> He then went into the second room where the little optimist was busily digging through the dung. He seemed excited and joyful, which baffled the psychologist. "Why are you so happy?" asked the psychologist.
>
> "Well," replied the little optimist, "with all this manure there just has to be a pony in here someplace, and I'm going to find it!"

Howard Clinebell, Ph.D., a pastoral psychotherapist, once said, "If you're given a six-foot plot of earth you either plant a garden or dig a grave." Our attitudes are a choice. The attitudes we teach our children are the attitudes we choose to teach. The one freedom that we have, according to Alfred Adler, is to choose our attitude in any given circumstance.

LACK OF PARENTING EDUCATION

> Question: Who taught us to parent? Who taught our parents to parent? Who taught their parents to parent?
>
> Answer: Our parents, their parents, and their parents' parents.

High school home economics teaches cooking, sewing, budgeting, home management, and etiquette. Hygiene classes teach personal cleanliness and health care. Sex education classes teach procreation and responsible sexuality. Our education system is designed to produce responsible young adults for entry into the world as contributing citizens.

But what about parenting education? Who teaches teenagers how to be parents? Who teaches them about infant care, child development, and stages of behavior? Who teaches alternatives to corporal punishment? Corporal punishment in the school system supports child abuse and contributes to the problems of family violence we're facing today.

Dr. Murray Straus says that "we need programs to help parents learn how to manage children without spanking."

Spanking a child is totally unnecessary.

On "The Oprah Winfrey Show," February 7, 1990, the panel consisted of four women who had been involved in varying forms of family violence. One panel member had stood by as her boyfriend threw her child up to the ceiling, and the child hit the floor so hard that she is now a paraplegic for life! The mother had been beaten several times by this man and had watched him abuse her children repeatedly. The audience participation and reactions were fascinating. One woman stood to speak with visible rage and piety, saying that she would never do such a thing to her children. She said, "I spank them, but that's it. I draw the line." One panel member told her that spanking is a form of abuse, and she angrily shouted back, "Oh no it isn't. Children need discipline!"

Children also need encouragement! Discipline can be experienced without physical punishment. The parent who is well educated in parenting skills and child development does not need to spank.

As this well-meaning mother defended spanking, I noticed anger in her voice and eyes. I could imagine this same anger through her inner child's eyes as she received a "healthy" spanking from her parents. Spanking, in the 1990s, does not make sense and is no longer acceptable. Many better and more effective methods are available for teaching children responsible boundaries and acceptable behaviors.

We must understand that the potential for violence exists within each of us and our choices between nonviolence and violence are our conscious responsibility. Once we accept this responsibility, we can then proceed with education, getting into recovery for alcohol or other drug abuse, lobbying for healthier television and screen programming, accomplishing stress management, and simply saying no to violence. Period.

Abusers can be your friends, your neighbors, your relatives. They are ordinary people caught in life situations beyond their control who do not know how to cope. Often they are isolated, having few close friends or family to give emotional support. In many cases, they were abused as children; and since this is the only kind of parenting they understand, they repeat it with their own children. Abuse occurs among all categories of economic levels, race, sex, ethnic heritage, and religion.

Albert Einstein once said, "You cannot solve a problem if you are thinking the same way you were thinking when you first created the problem."

We must become deciders and designers of our behavior. Instead of letting life happen to us, we must take a stand for happening to life! Oprah Winfrey is doing something about it. Her frustration on this particular program was visible, but she didn't get caught in the morass. She set a great example for all of us who want to stop family violence— she repeatedly took a stand for stopping it. Her intensity must be matched by ours!

CAUSES OF INCEST

Incest is the ultimate breakdown of family boundaries and mental health. The home is the environment in which children have the opportunity to grow and learn. The home is where children develop sexually, and healthy parenting is the top priority. Children must feel safe to explore, play, and develop.

When incest occurs, it turns the child's life upside down, inside out. Boundaries are shattered, trust is destroyed, fear is instilled forever, and a private rage is born. The world becomes a psychotic experience, one focused only on survival and confusion. If children aren't safe with their parents, they cannot feel safe with the world! Authority figures are automatically distrusted and become the objects of projected anger and fear.

The most common incest, and perhaps the most devastating, is between father and daughter. Think of it—the most important man in your life, your father, asking you to do things that seem wrong, using you for his own selfish pleasure. A father's responsibility with his daughters is to encourage their sexual maturing, not to destroy it. The little girl moving into puberty tests her newly developing characteristics by becoming naturally playful and focused on her father. His job is to affirm her as a person and let her know that her beauty includes sexuality but isn't the only thing beautiful about her.

According to research, five family conditions contribute to father-daughter incest:

1. emergence of the daughter as the central female figure of the household, in some respects taking over the role of the mother;

2. relative sexual incompatibility of the parents;

3. unwillingness of the father to seek a partner outside the nuclear family;

4. pervasive fears of abandonment and family disintegration, such that the family is desperately seeking an alternative to disintegration; and

5. unconscious sanction by the mother, who condones or fosters the assumption by the daughter of a sexual role with the father.[19]

The typical profile of the incestuous parent contains the following characteristics:

1. a history of promiscuity and diffuse sexual boundaries;

2. a history of alcohol and drug abuse;

3. a bad marriage in which father and mother avoid sexual expression and do not have a satisfying relationship;

4. a history of sexual abuse as a child;

5. addiction to pornographic materials;

6. social isolation;

7. a pattern of parental absence—where one parent is away from the home for lengthy periods of time.[20]

"In a study of older women victimized by incest as children, all of the women identified the inadequate relationship with their mother[s] as the most long lasting and destructive element of the experience."[21] Incest is less likely to occur when parents enjoy a mutually satisfying relationship.

In discussing some major causes of family violence, the reader becomes acutely aware of complications involved. One does not have to understand the causes in order to stop the violence. It's helpful information and lends insight into the dynamics of violence, but the abuser does not even have to admit that he has a problem in order to get help.

The bottom line on stopping family violence is intervention, *with or without the cooperation of the abuser* and with or without an understanding of causes. You don't have to know why you're being abused. You don't have to understand the causes. You only have to know that you do not deserve to be abused and you have to be willing to take immediate action to stop it. If you are aware of a family member or neighbor who is being abusive, you do not have to know why he or she is being abusive and you do not need to understand the causes. All you need to know is how to make an appropriate intervention and be willing to get involved!

NOTES

1. Georgia Council on Child Abuse, brochure, 1990.

2. S. K. Steinmetz, *Family Violence, Past, Present, Future* (Newark: University of Delaware, 1971), p. 752.

3. A. W. Schaef, "We're a Nation of Addicts," *New Age Journal*, March·April 1987, p. 47.

4. New Beginnings Marriage and Family Therapy (Athens, Ga., 1989).

5. J. G. Woititz, *Adult Children of Alcoholics* (Pompano Beach, Fla.: Health Communications, 1983), p. 4.

6. P. Cochran and M. Young, *The Violent Mind* (Pleasantville, N.Y.: Human Relations Media, 1982), p. 5.

7. Ibid.

8. Ibid.

9. T. Radecki, "War Games," *NCTV News*, vol. 10, (November 1989 to January 1990), p. 3.

10. Ibid.

11. Ibid.

12. Ibid.

13. Ibid.

14. Bob Dart, "Violence Saturates Children's Television," *Atlanta Journal/Constitution*, January 26, 1990.

15. *NCTV News*, vol. 5, nos. 3·4 (Washington, D.C., March·April 1984), p. 1.

16. Nielsen Index.

17. R. May, *Power and Innocence* (New York: Dell, 1972), p. 23.

18. *Atlanta Journal/Constitution*, January 25, 1990.

19. "Child Sexual Abuse: Incest, Assault, and Sexual Exploitation," United States Department of Health and Human Services.

20. Ibid.

21. Ibid.

3

STOPPING THE VIOLENCE

IF YOU ARE BEING ABUSED

The first step is to admit to yourself that you are being abused and that you deserve to be treated with respect. You have the right to feel safe from physical harm, especially in your own home.

Admit that violence is a problem within your family. I have heard abused women say many times, "He doesn't hit me all the time...maybe once or twice a month. The rest of the time is pretty good."

"He's really a very nice person, very caring. It's just a problem when he's mad, and that's not every day."

"I love him so much. I know he doesn't really mean to hurt me."

Until a person addicted to alcohol is able to say, "I'm an alcoholic," treatment prognosis is extremely poor. Usually it takes being sick and tired of being sick and tired. The same is true if you're being abused. Until you can say, "I'm a victim of spouse abuse," it is very likely that you'll continue to be a victim.

Emergency actions. If you're being abused, you need to take immediate action. My main advice is to *get out*. Leave the premises. This may be a problem because of feeling trapped or afraid for your children. You can hide extra car keys and money in an easily accessible place. Just as individuals make escape plans in case of fire, you need to have an escape plan for family violence. Arrange for a place to go in an emergency. Choose a place your spouse doesn't know. Many metropolitan areas offer shelters for battered spouses and can provide free room and board for several days.

45

If your spouse becomes violent, defend yourself as best you can. As soon as you are able, leave—with your children. If you're unable to get out, call 911 or the police (often 911 is the police number). Memorize these numbers and have them written down near the phone.

If at all possible, get out fast! And don't go back! Violent outbursts and abusive behavior only get worse without intervention and rehabilitation. Don't let your spouse sweet-talk you with remorseful begging and promises that it will never happen again. Without intervention, it will!

Get professional help. Talk to someone about the problem. You probably are listening to some old, self-defeating internal messages about being abused. Our thoughts, memories, and internal monologues are actually conversations within ourselves. As long as you accept those old, self-defeating conversations, change is not likely to occur. Abused spouses need to develop new beliefs about themselves. In the book *Stopping Wife Abuse*, by Jennifer Baker Fleming, the following attitudes are suggested as positive and useful new internal monologues:

- I am not to blame for being beaten and abused.
- I am not the cause of another's violent behavior.
- I do not like it or want it.
- I do not have to take it.
- I am an important human being.
- I am a worthwhile woman.
- I deserve to be treated with respect.
- I do have power over my own life.
- I can make changes in my life if I want to.
- I am not alone. I can ask others to help me.
- I am worth working for and changing for.
- I deserve to make my own life safe and happy.[1]

Family violence is often a well-kept secret. Healing will begin if you talk about the secret(s). A professional family therapist who is trained in family violence can help. Community supported agencies can provide family therapy on a sliding fee scale if finances are a problem for you. (More specific information on how to select a therapist is given in the conclusion of chapter 4.)

Dr. Susan Forward, in her book *Toxic Parents*, refers to alcoholism in the family as the "dinosaur in the living room" that no one talks about. "To an outsider the dinosaur is impossible to ignore, but for those within the home, the hopelessness of evicting the beast forces them to pretend it isn't there." Family violence is a dinosaur in every room of the house, and every family member is afraid to talk about it. It becomes the family secret, and the power of a secret is in the "not telling." A secret loses its power when told, and if you want the dinosaur out of the house, you're going to have to talk about it and face up to it.[2]

It really is okay to tell. In fact, it is your best hope! If you keep the abuse silent and secret, it will continue and it will get worse.

When a perpetrator of spouse abuse actually makes it to therapy, court ordered or voluntarily, he often will stop the abuse simply by being told to do so. Once the abuse is public knowledge, it often stops. It is imperative that you tell those you trust—friends, family neighbors, your church. Then seek professional help that can provide supportive intervention in a rehabilitating way.

Join support groups that are available in your community. Shelters for battered spouses and community mental health agencies can provide information about local groups. Departments of family and children's services provide such programs as "Mother's Day Out." Familiarize yourself with what's available.

Take legal action. If your spouse will not stop the violence, take out a civil protection order. If you have been abused and the police have been called, follow through by testifying in court. Love is no excuse for accepting physical or emotional abuse. In most states, law enforcement officials are required to make an arrest where domestic violence has occurred.

I understand any reluctance on your part to call for help. If you've had bad experiences in calling the authorities in the past, keep in mind that all over the country, police academies have prioritized family violence. If you are unlucky enough to get a prejudiced officer who treats you in a "less than" way, get his or her name and badge number and call your local police headquarters to report the incident.

You not only deserve respect and nonviolence from your spouse, you deserve respect and help from your local law enforcement agency.

In the early 1970s, a police officer had to actually witness the abuse to make an arrest. If arriving on the scene after the abuse had occurred, he or she could only advise the victim to swear out a warrant and—in some cases—stand by for protection while the abused person safely left the scene. With the passing of new legislation, all you have to do is tell the officer that your spouse or boyfriend hit you and an arrest can be made under family violence codes.

Spouse abuse and child abuse evoke the deepest of emotions in our law enforcement personnel. When I was a young police officer, I handled the arrest of a young mother in Atlanta who had dropped her baby onto the freeway from an overpass. I hated her. I felt nothing but contempt and rage toward her. Police officers who come into your home and see your bruises, cuts, and pain are human beings. They have feelings, too. The toughest case to handle is child abuse, especially when it's severe. The officer is to maintain professionalism while protecting people from harm. It's a tough job, and sometimes they simply break down.

Imagine having to go in and make an arrest on Lattie's mother and live-in boyfriend in the following situation.

Chicago—Lattie McGee, age 4, was a tortured prisoner in his own home. His cell was a dark closet in his family's South Side apartment, where he often was hung upside down, bound and gagged for hours. Lattie was starved, burned with a hot iron, stuck with pins and needles, singed with cigarettes, beaten with a tree branch, hair brush, belt and hands, scalded with steaming water and tied up . . . for two-and-a-half months the summer of '87. A severe blow to his head was the eventual cause of death, but his emaciated body, scarred from head to foot, was so infected from untreated wounds that he likely would have died a short time later. His pelvis had been broken several days before he died, and two of his ribs had been snapped several weeks earlier.

Lattie's mother and her live-in boyfriend, who said he beat Lattie and his brother because he thought they were homosexual, are to be sentenced Thursday by Cook County Criminal Court Judge Michael B. Getty.

—Lindsay Tanner, Associated Press,
Atlanta Journal/Constitution, **February 11, 1990.**

This little boy's mother, Alicia Abraham, twenty-eight, acknowledged that she had never reported the torture of her children but said she did not abuse them herself! She did torture her children by not reporting the abuse. She is as guilty as her boyfriend, and just as sick! This book is not for people who are that sick. This book is for individuals who are seeking an end to violence in their lives and are willing and able to get the rehabilitative help required for healing.[3]

I take a firm stand on family violence. There is no gray area, no compromise. It must stop, and you must help stop it. Also take the stand that if you don't stop it, then society has the responsibility to intervene and stop it for you—with or without your cooperation. One of the guests on Oprah Winfrey's show remorsefully said of her years of abusing her children, "No one ever bothered to intervene!"

The bottom line on family violence is intervention. You must stop it wherever you can. The first time is the beginning of the habit. Walk out the first time—period! Do not stay and see if it won't happen again. It will. I cannot stress that enough! It will not get better by staying in it.

Divorce him and move on. If your spouse refuses professional help or doesn't make progress even if he does get professional help, divorce him and move on! The day of staying in the marriage to be a loyal, subservient martyr is over. Nobody, not one creature of God's creation, deserves to be beaten and abused. And before you marry again, be certain that you have sufficiently worked through the issues that influenced your mate selection in the first place. What is it that you can be more aware of the second time around? How can you tell if your boyfriend is a potential abuser?

I encourage my clients to actually interview any person of the opposite sex with whom they are becoming seriously involved. You can learn how to complete a family life assessment that provides valuable information about behavioral patterns, learned behaviors and addictions, and predictive indicators of possible violence.

For example, ask him what it was like growing up in his family. This question opens the door to a lot of information. Keep in mind all of the information that you have learned about family violence in the first two chapters. Listen for any abuse—mental or physical—in the relationships described, that is, of siblings, parents, friends, neighbors, or animals.

Ask if he was ever abused as a child. If he was, he is very likely to be abusive to you or your children. Has he worked on these problems in therapy? Most adult survivors of child abuse need professional coaching to heal the deep wounds.

Ask if he witnessed his parents physically fighting or yelling at each other. If he did, the probability of his resolving conflict in the same manner with you is very likely. If he hedges on this, pay attention to how he handles stress and conflict while you're dating. Pay attention to how he relates to his parents, siblings, and other people. Sooner or later, he probably will treat you the same way.

Is there any history of alcohol or drug abuse in his family? Though not the cause of violence, substance abuse contributes significantly to the potential for abusive behavior. If the answer is yes, then ask if he abuses alcohol or drugs. If this answer is yes or evasive, ask him to get into recovery before any further plans are made about your relationship! If he refuses, get out of the relationship, return to go, and collect a high amount of self-esteem for making a great decision on behalf of your well-being!

Ask if there is any history of family violence. Since people are so reluctant to admit to this "dinosaur in the living room," you'll need to listen to his body language as well as his words. If you learn of any indication of family violence, proceed—if at all—with extreme caution. An old adage is that if you want to know how a man is going to treat his wife, watch how he treats his sister and his mother. Also, when you're visiting in his home, pay attention to how his father treats his mother and sisters. All of this is valuable information.

Ask him how his parents disciplined him as a child. This will give you important information on how he views discipline. If his parents used a paddle or rod, he may believe in using a paddle or rod on your children.

Ask him if he has ever used violence in resolving conflict. If so, you're in for trouble. If he has been violent before, you must be prepared for him eventually to become violent with you.

If he's been married before, ask if there was any violence involved in that relationship. Be specific. If they have children, ask how they discipline(d) them. These are obvious questions.

You may be thinking, "I would never ask such direct questions." But with a woman being beaten every fifteen seconds in the United States and six million children being physically abused every year, you need to know about your potential partner.

If any one of the answers to the above questions is affirmative, proceed with extreme caution. Seek premarital counseling with a fam-

50

ily therapist trained in family violence. You are very likely heading into an abusive relationship. No matter how peaceful and calm it seems during courtship, the worm turns after the "I do." You want to know, "I do what?"

The following is a profile of the man who batters:

- Has a low tolerance for stressful situations.
- Rarely shows emotions or talks about his feelings.
- Has low self-esteem and lacks self-confidence.
- Tends to abuse alcohol and other drugs.
- Sees himself as a failure.
- Is extremely dependent on his marriage relationship; he needs it for security.
- Is extremely jealous and possessive.
- Is generally fascinated with guns and weapons of violence.
- Has unrealistic expectations about life, his mate, and their children.
- Is angry at the world.
- Probably was battered as a child.
- Probably witnessed his father beating his mother and siblings.
- May become severely depressed and use remorse to keep the victim imprisoned in the battering relationship.
- Rarely acknowledges the seriousness of his behavior.

Men aren't the only ones who batter their spouses. One of my clients complained that his wife had the bad habit of literally punching him in the face with her fist. She was a strong woman and one time actually knocked him out. He did not abuse her. He was confused and ashamed, expressing the basic symptoms of an abused woman.

If your spouse is abusing you, let's review what to do.

1. The first step in breaking the habit of family violence is to admit that it is a serious problem.

2. Take emergency action. If you're being abused, you need to take immediate action. My main advice is to get out, leave the premises. Go to a shelter for battered women.

3. Get professional help. Talk to someone about the problem.

4. Join support groups that are available in your community.

5. Take legal action. If your spouse will not stop the violence and you feel threatened, take out a civil protection order. If you have been abused and the police have been called, follow through by testifying in court.

6. Divorce him! If your spouse refuses professional help or doesn't make progress even if he does get professional help, divorce him and move on!

IF YOUR PARENTS ARE ABUSING YOU

The National Child Abuse Hotline is:
1-800-4 A CHILD.

If your parents are abusing you, you are probably very angry, scared, and hurt. Although it is difficult, you can help the situation if you will do some very important things.* First, read this section very carefully and then decide what you want to do about the problem.

That's right, *you have decision power*—tough as it may seem—to do something about being abused.

Young people who are abused get back at their parent or parents by acting out their anger. Anytime someone hits you or forces you to do things that are harmful to you, you become angry and decrease your trust in that person. Some acting out is very dangerous and self-destructive. Avoid doing anything harmful to yourself, your parents, or anyone else. The following recommendations are given with you and your family's best interests in mind.

The abuse is not your fault! The first and most important thing for you to know about being abused is that it isn't your fault! Abused kids get it into their heads that there must be something wrong with them for their parent(s) or relative(s) to be abusing them: "It can't be because my parents are sick or don't love me, so there must be something wrong with me."

* Young children will not likely be reading this book. The author is addressing older adolescents and teenagers in this section. Young children who are being abused will need adult intervention (see page 65).

I want you to know that there is nothing wrong with you. You are okay! Whoever is hurting and harming you is not okay. They need help, and they won't get it unless you tell somebody who can help.

Most young people are afraid to do anything about being abused for fear of breaking up their family or getting into deeper trouble with the abusing parent. These fears are understandable because even when you are hit and hurt, you probably still love your parents. It is confusing when they hurt you, but the good times may seem to make up for the bad times.

You also may be afraid to talk to anyone about what is happening because of being threatened or told that certain things will happen if you tell. Some of the things you may have been told are:

- If you talk to anyone, I'll beat the daylights out of you!
- If you talk, no one will believe your word against mine.
- If you talk to your mother, she will get very angry with you.
- If you talk, they'll probably take you away from me, and you won't live here anymore.
- If you talk to the neighbors, they'll think that there's something wrong with you.
- If you talk, your mother will divorce me, and that will break up our home.
- If you talk, you will be in deep trouble.

Despite these kinds of threats or thoughts, if you're being abused physically, emotionally, or sexually, tell somebody.

If you're being abused, tell someone you trust. Choose carefully whom you confide in. The problem is not going to get better, and it's not going to go away. You have a right to life, liberty, and the pursuit of happiness. Abusive parents or adults take these away and literally rob you of your future. What's happening to you is not a private family problem. It is a public social problem. Nobody has the right to hit or harm you in any way.

Whom do you tell? This is a tough one. If you tell another family member, they may not believe you or they may tell the abusing parent; and then you're right back where you started, with an angry parent. Select someone whom you trust, an adult who can help. This *may* be a family member, but not likely. Abuse runs in families, and whoever is abusing you probably learned it from his or her parents. Aunts, uncles, grandparents, and parents are all likely to be unsympathetic to your plight. They may even support what is happening to you as God's will or the way to parent, or believe that you deserve it—whatever "it" may be.

If you choose a family member and nothing is done about the abuse, or if he or she tells your abusive parent(s) and the abuse gets worse, talk to someone in the helping professions. They are mandated by law to report any known cases of child abuse. Choose a school counselor, teacher, school social worker or nurse, minister, priest, rabbi, doctor, or lawyer. If you live near a community mental health center, that may be an excellent source for help.

If you talk with one of these professionals and do not get satisfactory results, go to someone else. Don't give up! Before you say anything else, ask your choice of confidant(e) what he or she believes about family violence and child abuse. If the response includes anything like "but I believe a parent has the right to physical punishment," find someone else. Find someone who will help. It may take courage and persistence. But it's a matter of degree—you can do it!

If you know of no one you can trust, call child protective services. Your area has a hotline you can call. If you don't know what the number is, call information. Your operator can help with this, too. Shelters and emergency foster care are available for victims of family violence. Remember, the National Child Abuse Hotline is: 1-800-4 A CHILD.

If abuse is imminent, get out and go to a safe place to call. If you call from home, your abusing parent may hear you and become more violent. If you're not in imminent danger, wait until the next day and call from school or work. If you can't stay at a friend's until the next day and you feel threatened, do everything you can to protect yourself: barricade your door and have an emergency exit plan.

Help is available, but you have to take the first step. Nobody can help if he or she doesn't know.

Once you tell, state the truth and stay with the truth. Don't change your story under pressure or fear! Once the abuse is out in the open, you may experience a lot of pressure from your abusing parent to change your story, to save them from embarrassment, to lie. They may even threaten you. Don't lie! Stay with the truth and nothing but the truth, no matter what anyone says or advises. The truth will get the help that you deserve. It will stop the abuse that you don't deserve.

We all have scars from our childhood. Some we wear on the outside; most we wear on the inside. You're not alone. Over six million children are severely assaulted by family members every year in the United States. Many areas of the country have child abuse support groups where you can share with other teenagers. Getting help now is an investment in your future.

It is important for you to know that not every family is like yours. It is not okay to be abusive and violent. You have rights. You are an important citizen, a VIP (very important person) who holds the future of our society in your development as a healthy, empowered young man or woman. You are valuable and deserve help. With all the other people of this world who are committed to stopping family violence, I stand for you and with you in stopping your abuse.[4]

IF YOUR CHILDREN ARE BEING ABUSED

Most parents know when their children are being abused by the other parent. They may not know, however, when their child is being abused by other family members. It is very important to pay attention to children's messages about this. Children do not come up to the nonabusing parent and say, "I am being abused," or "Uncle Zeke rubs my genitals when I visit him on the weekends." Instead, children are very indirect and often ashamed of what's happening. They feel like it's their fault, and they are scared. However, we can decipher their elusive messages if we're paying attention.

"I don't want to see Daddy anymore" is a strong communication that something is wrong. Or, "Please, Mommy, don't make me go to Grandpa's house ever again," or "I don't like Mrs. Smith [the Cub Scout leader]; I don't want to go camping with her again."

If not in words, you can notice actions—bed-wetting, screaming nightmares, stealing, severe withdrawal and depression, asthma, preoccupation with genitals, sudden drop in school performance, crying hysterically for no apparent reason—and many other ways of communicating that something very damaging has happened or is happening to them. A teenager will display different communications—promiscuity, alcohol and other drug abuse, violent behaviors, self-destructive risk-taking, running away, and, worst of all, depression and suicidal thoughts or attempts.

Each day, eighteen teenagers commit suicide in the United States. That's 6,570 teenage suicides a year.[5]

If you're aware that your child is being abused, make it stop!

Pay attention to your kids and believe them. We must pay attention to our kids and make certain that we provide every opportunity for open communication about what is happening in their lives. Understand that "suicide is the period at the end of a sentence that no one has read."[6]

Don't ignore abuse. There is no such thing as a nonabusing parent who knows about the abuse and does nothing to stop it. The passive mother who silently disapproves of the violent beatings given out by her husband is just as responsible for the brutality as he is. If you're a spectator, you're a participant in the abuse.

Do something about it. Many mothers do not know of the abuse. Once they do, the next step is to do something about it. If a parent ignores abuse, he or she becomes a party to the abuse. If your child begs you not to make him go back to visit his stepmother and you force him to anyway, you are responsible for both your child and your decision. If you learn later that she has been molesting your child, you are also responsible for that abuse. Parents have the responsibility to protect their children. If you don't protect your child, who will? Listen carefully to your children's communications and concerns. They may be telling you something that they're afraid for you or anybody to hear, but it is also something they want stopped and need your help to stop it!

Stop the violence. Talk to the offending parent or family member. Do this at a time when the offender is calm and rational. However, if you should catch the other person in the act, whether it be a beating or incestuous action, intervene immediately. Call the police and do whatever else is necessary to interrupt the brutality and protect your child. Chances are, this will be quite dangerous and you will be at risk. You'll have to decide how best to intervene. Frankly, if you're living with someone so violent that he would not stop when confronted, you and your kids need to be out of there "yesterday!" You've already waited too long.

When you talk to the other person, be direct and to the point. For example, tell your husband or ex-husband, "I want you to stop hitting our children. I want you to make a commitment to stop what you've been doing, and together we will seek professional help."

If the other person denies what has been happening, seek immediate professional help. Family violence isn't a disease that you get help for when it's convenient to do so. Family violence is a disease that needs immediate attention and intervention, voluntarily or involuntarily.[7] If the abuse isn't stopped by talking to the offender, call the police.

If your spouse or family member doesn't stop the abuse, call the police and leave with your children—if possible. The abuser may not listen to you but may respond to an objective outsider, an authority figure. The police also will provide temporary protection for you and your children while you seek more long-lasting help.

Call a family therapist for an emergency session; get professional help. Child abuse is a problem that is rarely self-cured. Professional intervention with the abuser and supportive coaching for the victim(s), including the nonabusing parent, is needed. Very few parents call departments of family and children's services for help with child abuse. You may feel more comfortable in calling a family therapist for an emergency session. He or she will help make any necessary contact with agencies.

When people first come into a therapist's office in the middle of a crisis, their lives are basically out of control. Most people who are out of control want help. There is a natural tendency to rely on the control of the professional in order to reestablish some sense of stability. The crisis intervention specialist's job is to establish and maintain control throughout the crisis. When the crisis is past, control is given back to the client, who's ready to practice what has been learned in therapy.

Sounds simple, and it is. I have found that at least 85 percent of the abusing parents or spouses with whom I have worked in the last fifteen years actually will stop the abuse when advised or told to do so. It is often a relief to have the family secret out in the open and to respond to a helping authority's request or demand to stop the violence.

"It is wrong to hit a woman," I told one client. "Hasn't anyone ever taught you that?"

His response was, "Well, no, I've always thought you were supposed to."

He stopped hitting his wife. Together, during six months of intense marriage therapy and conflict resolution training, they built a nonviolent relationship that worked.

If a spouse is resistant to therapy or the request to stop the abuse, then the therapist actually can demand it with a mandated report to the authorities. When child abuse has occurred, a therapist is mandated by law to report it.

If your spouse or family member refuses therapy, then you will need to report the abuse yourself, or talk to a professional in your community who can make the report for you. Talk to your clergy, doctor, nurse, or a family therapist. For your children's sake, get help, with or without your spouse.

If the abuse is sexual, don't neglect doing any of the following:

1. First and foremost, believe your child. Children rarely lie about being sexually abused. It isn't something they would talk about if it wasn't happening. Younger children do not have the vocabulary of sexual knowledge that an adult sexual offender has. When they become descriptive, it's because they've learned it.

2. Control your own reactions to the news. Your angry emotions can overwhelm the already overwhelmed child. Sympathize with your child, listening to her or his feelings and thoughts. Make certain that your child knows you don't blame him or her. Give emotional support.

3. Take your child immediately to the emergency room of your local hospital for an examination of any injuries. The attending physician will document a report and—together with you—contact the authorities.

4. Make certain that the proper authorities have been notified. They will help you find professional help and ensure the safety of your child. Remember, if you don't report it, then you become a participant in the abuse. The person abusing your child will abuse other children, too. And he or she will likely abuse your child again and again, until you stop it!

If your spouse is sexually abusing your child, immediately separate from him. Do not remove the child from the home unless you go with her or him. A child who is removed from the home after telling about being abused associates the removal with being responsible. The child may think that he has done something wrong: "There must be something wrong with me to get kicked out while my father gets to stay at home."

It is imperative that you get the abuser out of the home immediately. A child who has been sexually assaulted or manipulated by a parent will live in fear of that parent regardless of how much rehabilitation the offender accomplishes.

When parents sexually use their children for selfish pleasure, they surrender the right to be that child's role model in life. They shatter boundaries and instill confusion and personality dissolution. Incest is a form of violence that breaks down the family unit.

Separation of the offender from the home for a lengthy period of time allows the opportunity for supervised visitation, extensive therapeutic education, and time for the family to decide if it wants to be together again. Divorce may be the healthiest option, with limited visitation rights, if any. A strictly supervised contract is required with the offender, much the same as being on probation or parole. The child must feel protected and safe in order to be in a relationship with the offending parent(s).

If the offender is a sibling, the options are narrowed. The simplest choice is to educate the entire family in what is normal, acceptable behavior and what isn't. Clear consequences of dysfunctional behavior need to be stated and followed. Parents will need to deal with their absentia and setting healthy boundaries in the family. The sibling will need to learn that incest is taboo and totally unacceptable. He will need to know that it is a social problem and not a private family affair. The victim will need to know that the abuse will stop and that keen parental observation and intervention will be practiced. Siblings will need to reconcile and put the behavior in the past. Family therapy is a must and will provide monitoring and sex education both outside and inside the family.

If the offender is an extended family member, such as an uncle or grandparent, limit visits (if any) to those that are completely supervised. *Never, never* leave that relative and the child alone. Send a strong message that all behavior is being closely monitored and that no further abuse will be tolerated.

IF YOU ARE ABUSING YOUR SPOUSE OR A FAMILY MEMBER

Get professional help. The violence must stop! For your sake and—more important—your family's sake, seek professional help. If you are violently losing your temper a lot and do not get the help you need, it will only get worse. You may seriously injure your spouse or child and eventually lose your family through death, divorce, separation, or incarceration.

In our current society, it is very likely that you will be reported and that a caseworker from a department of social services will contact you to initiate immediate intervention to stop the violence. Family violence is a crime. It is against the laws of our society to commit aggravated or simple assault on your children, spouse, or any other family member. Incarceration may not be the best choice, but it may be the ultimate social response to what you are doing.

Treatment is the smartest choice. It can keep the family together and facilitate healing of the deep wounds inflicted by your violence. You can learn new and better ways of parenting and being intimate with your spouse.

You probably are doing what you learned to do and repeating what was done to you as a child. Your parents probably were repeating what they had learned, and so on, back through the generations of unskilled parenting and enslaving ideas about women and children. Women and children are not second-class citizens to be used and abused for man's convenience. We are all partners in life; our children are separate citizens with equal rights and needs. Our parents may have been doing the best they knew by physically punishing us.

**Our parents' best intentions and actions in the past
are not good enough for the present.**

Our task is to improve on past generations. We know today that hitting another human being always sets up angry reactions and breakdowns in the relationship. Professional help can provide marriage enrichment, nonviolent conflict management, and parenting skills that work. Get help before it's too late. Your children need you. They need you to be an adequate, caring, nurturing parent who chooses to be in recovery.

A recovering parent named Marcellus Leona writes:

THE ABUSE STOPS HERE!

I remember the day my mother was visiting and my one-year-old child decided to investigate the decorative antique glassware on our coffee table. After attempting to distract her several times with a more interesting toy, I gave up and moved the glassware out of reach. My mother said, "Just smack her on the hand a few times and she'll get the message. That's what I did to you."

And get the message I did. I was suddenly aware of where I had learned to scream at and hit my children. Of course, I never scream so loud or as often as she did, nor do I smack my children in the mouth every time their words are disrespectful. I haven't hit them on their heads with telephone receivers. I've only hit them on their bottoms with my hand and physically shaken them when they really misbehaved.

At that moment everything became clear to me. That this violent behavior toward my children was so ingrained in my being that I wasn't even aware of it. I knew how badly it made me feel as a child, but I didn't know of a kinder, gentler world of disciplining children. I only knew what my experience was, and it must have been right because it was my mother doing it.

With this new awareness I set out to stop it, and I have! It was an awesome responsibility to take on the task of changing parenting habits that have been entrenched in our family for over 150 years. I sought the help of a family therapist, himself a recovering adult survivor of childhood parental abuse. With his coaching I have taken "Active Parenting" classes and have read several books about anger, violence, parenting, being an adult child of an alcoholic, codependency, and child abuse. I joined a support group of other recover-

ing parents, began an exercise program for reducing my stress level, and joined the local Council on Child Abuse. I also became a sponsor, a support person for another abusive mother.

One of the most important things I did was to focus on my marriage instead of dumping my frustrations onto my children. Now when I say "I'm a good mother," I BELIEVE IT! I know that I will not leave a legacy of violence for my children to carry on. THE ABUSE STOPS HERE!

Remember, violence is a learned behavior. New behaviors for resolving conflict can be learned. Like any new behavioral skill, they will need to be practiced over and over. Old habits die hard! Even someone as committed as Marcellus Leona needed coaching and practice. As Mark Twain once said, "Habit is habit, and not to be flung out of the window by any man, but coaxed downstairs a step at a time."

Stop the violence. After calling for an appointment to get professional help, make a commitment to stop the violence. Practice "time-outs" on yourself. Separate from stressful situations with your spouse and children. If you need to, move out temporarily until you can begin recovery. If you stay in the home and feel yourself getting angry, withdraw, take a walk, go jogging—do anything constructive, nothing destructive. Have a designated friend whom you can call and talk to when you're feeling stressed and approaching a breaking point.

Talk to as many people as you can. Get it out in the open. Violent behavior is learned and becomes habitual. If kept secret, it gets worse. Public confession and announcement of getting into recovery is a big first step to breaking the habit. I have revised the Twelve Steps of Alcoholics Anonymous (AA) for family violence. Read these every morning and evening and add the serenity prayer by Reinhold Niebuhr that follows these Twelve Steps.

Twelve Steps of Recovery from Family Violence

1. I claim responsibility for my violence and admit that my life has become unmanageable.

2. I came to the awareness that I have the power and resources to restore my life to socially acceptable nonviolent behavior.

3. I made a decision to include the care of God, as I understand God to be, in my life and recovery.

4. I made a complete examination of myself and how I learned to be violent.

5. I admitted to God, to myself, and to other human beings the exact nature of my violent behaviors.

6. I became entirely ready to do everything that is necessary and required to change my being and to stop the violence.

7. I humbly asked God for forgiveness and the courage to recover and learn a new way of being.

8. I made a list of all persons I have harmed and became willing to make amends to them all, except when to do so would injure them or others.

9. I continue to monitor my thoughts, fantasies, and behaviors and make immediate changes when they're counterproductive.

10. I sought, through reconciliation and recovery, improved relationships of open honesty and trust.

11. I have joined support groups (like Parents Anonymous) and continue to talk openly about my violent behaviors and recovery.

12. Having had a "turning around" of my life, I will share this experience with others prone to violence and practice these principles in all our conversations and actions.

> **"God grant me the serenity to accept the things I cannot change, courage to change the things I can and wisdom to know the difference." Amen.**
> **—Reinhold Niebuhr**

Know that intervention is on the way. If you don't seek help voluntarily, intervention from outside resources is likely to occur. Thankfully, our society is reporting family violence. People talk! Sooner or later—hopefully sooner—your violence will be reported to the authorities. It would be much better for you to seek help of your own free will.

However, if you don't seek professional help and are reported, the results are determined by your state laws. In Georgia, for example, code section 27-207 amended, section 4. (a) reads:

> **The court may, upon the filing of a verified petition, grant any protective order or approve any consent agreement to bring about a cessation of acts of family violence. The order or agreements may:**
>
> **(1) Direct a party to refrain from such acts;**
>
> **(2) Grant to a spouse possession of the residence or household of the parties and exclude the other spouse from the residence or household;**
>
> **(3) Require a party to provide a spouse and his or her children suitable alternate housing;**
>
> **(4) Award temporary custody of minor children and establish temporary visitation rights;**
>
> **(5) Order the eviction of a party from the residence or household and assistance to the victim in returning to it or order assistance in retrieving personal property of the victim if the respondent's eviction has not been ordered;**
>
> **(6) Order either party to make payments for the support of a minor child as required by law;**
>
> **(7) Order either party to make payments for the support of a spouse as required by law;**
>
> **(8) Provide for possession of personal property of the parties;**
>
> **(9) Order a party to refrain from harassing or interfering with the other;**
>
> **(10) Award costs and attorney's fees to either party; and**
>
> **(11) Include any additional protections or provisions as deemed necessary.**

If the police are called to your residence in response to a neighbor's call or someone in your immediate household, an arrest can be made based on the Family Violence Act. All police officers need in Georgia, for example, is "probable cause to believe that an act of family violence has been committed, or for other cause there is likely to be failure of justice for want of an officer to issue a warrant" (code section 27-207 [a]).

Get the help you need. You are responsible for the violence, and you can be responsible for and participate in stopping it. One thing is certain: IT MUST STOP! It is not a private matter. It is a serious crime.

IF YOU ARE AWARE THAT YOUR FRIEND, NEIGHBOR, RELATIVE, OR CHILD IS BEING ABUSED

The National Child Abuse Hotline is: 1-800-4 A CHILD.

Get involved! Where it is possible, talk to the victim(s) and/or perpetrator. Family violence is not a private matter. It is a public matter. People caught in abuse—both victims and perpetrators—are habituated to their patterns of behavior and may not seek help on their own. If the victim is an adult, she may feel trapped and hopeless. You can be a link between her and the help she needs.

If the victims are children, regardless of age, they usually can't help themselves. Even if they knew what to do, they probably wouldn't do it. The only security and love they know is expressed in the violent home. They may perceive their home as normal and abuse as a way of life. They even may feel that they deserve the punishment, thinking they are bad children. Their parents can learn how to be nonviolent, and you can help make that happen.

How can one create the possibility of stopping violence? First, you may be able to talk directly to the victim(s) and encourage him or her to seek help. Many abusers also want help but don't know where to turn. Make your approach as nonthreatening as possible. You might say something like, "I've noticed you have been under a lot of stress lately. I've heard you screaming and the kids crying. Is there anything I can do to help?" This will open the door to conversation about what's been happening.

If the person is resistant or tells you to mind your own business, be polite but firm. Say something like this: "I understand how you feel, but I'm really concerned about you and your children. Let me know if ever I can help." If the person continues to be in denial and you see signs of child abuse, go home and report it. In many cases, however, you will find the person eager to talk to someone about the abuse.

You might give the abuser a copy of this book and suggest that the person see a family therapist. Be reassuring that help is available. Encourage them to call while you are with them. It's easier for them to postpone the task and stay in the old way of being than it is to call for help and begin a new, unknown path of recovery. Be compassionate and understanding, even when you are talking to a perpetrator of violence. They already feel bad enough and will react to judgment with strong defenses. Your goal is to encourage them to seek help.

After talking with your friend, neighbors, or relatives and encouraging them to get help, *report the abuse.* This is always a tough decision. But when parents are out of control, I always choose to protect the children—even at the risk of losing the adult relationship.

As a family therapist, I always inform the parents or individual that I am making a report as mandated by law and that I am available for family therapy if they choose to continue working with me to stop the violence. Some people never speak to me again. This is unfortunate, but my priority is concern for their children and stopping the violence. Others do speak to me after intervention and are thankful for having received the help they couldn't or wouldn't seek on their own.

You can make an anonymous report to local agencies that protect children. When calling, you will be asked to give substantial information that has led you to believe that abuse has occurred.

Be familiar with indicators of family violence. "Violent families demonstrate certain common characteristics. They live in closed systems. There is a firm commitment to maintain a tight boundary between the family and the outside world. A common rule is secrecy."[8]

Social isolation is a way of maintaining the family secret. Often the only people who have outside contact with a violent family are the family doctor, those in the school system or maybe in a church. It is imperative that teachers, medical personnel, and clergy know the indicators of child abuse and spouse abuse and be committed to reporting it.

Following are profiles, or indicators, of family violence:

Profile of physically abused or neglected children

- They appear to be different from other children in physical and emotional makeup or their parents describe them as being different or bad.

- They seem afraid of their parents.

- They may bear bruises, welts, sores, or other skin injuries.

- They are given inappropriate food, drink, or medication.

- They are left alone or with inadequate supervision.

- They are chronically unclean.

- They exhibit extremes in behavior: cry often or cry very little and show no real expectation of being comforted; they are excessively fearful or seem fearless of adult authority; they are unusually aggressive or extremely passive or withdrawn.

- They are wary of physical contact, especially with an adult. They may be hungry for affection yet have difficulty relating to children and adults. Based on their experiences, they feel they cannot risk getting close to others.

- They exhibit a sudden change in behavior, exhibit regressive behavior, such as wetting their pants or bed, thumb-sucking, whining, or becoming uncommonly shy or passive.

- They have learning problems that cannot be diagnosed. Their attention wanders and they easily become self-absorbed.

- They are habitually truant or late to school. Frequent or prolonged absences from school may result from the parent's keeping an injured child at home until the evidence of abuse disappears. Or they may arrive at school early and remain after classes instead of going home.

- They are dressed inappropriately for the weather. Children who wear long sleeves on hot days may be dressed to hide bruises or burns or other marks of abuse, or they may be dressed inadequately and suffer frostbite or illness from exposure to inclement weather.[9]

Profile of emotionally abused children

- Habits, such as biting, rocking, head-banging, or thumb-sucking in an older child or teen.
- Eating disorders.
- Daytime anxieties and unrealistic fears.
- Sleep disorders, nightmares.
- Enuresis (involuntary bed-wetting in an older child or teen).
- Speech disorders, such as stuttering and stammering.
- Withdrawn and antisocial behavior.
- Poor peer relationships.
- Distrustful and overly fearful of strangers.
- Irrational persistent fears, dreads, or hatreds.
- Hypochondria (abnormally anxious about her/his health or imagines she/he is ill).
- Low self-esteem (lacks self-confidence).
- Lack of creativity and healthy exploration; seems not to know how to play.
- Apathetic; feels little or no emotion; indifferent and listless.
- Lacks purpose and determination.
- Seems oblivious to hazards and risks.
- Destructive behaviors.
- Obsessive or compulsive behaviors.
- Behavior extremes; aggressive or passive-dependent; assumes the parent role with other children or is infantile; behavior is rigid or overly impulsive.
- Daydreams frequently; has hallucinations; overfantasizes; seems removed from reality.
- Academic failure in that the child does not achieve up to abilities; may seem almost mentally retarded.
- Sadomasochistic behavior (seems cruel and gets pleasure from hurting other children, adults, or animals; or conversely, seems to get pleasure from being mistreated).
- Self-destructive; may attempt suicide.[10]

From my clinical experience and from further studies on the topic, I have compiled a profile of the sexually abused child.

Profile of sexually abused children

- Withdrawal into fantasy worlds.

- Unusual knowledge and/or interest in sexual acts and terminology beyond their chronological age.

- Unusual seductiveness with classmates, teachers, or other adults.

- Sexual self-consciousness, provocativeness, or vulnerability to sexual approaches.

- Refusal to dress for physical education.

- Extreme fear of showers and/or rest rooms (these are common places for sexual abuse to occur).

- Frequent absences from school that are justified by only one parent.

- Repeated attempts to run away from home.

- Reluctance or fear of going home after school or early arrival every day for no apparent reason.

- Depiction of unusual or bizarre sexual themes in art work or stories beyond age-level development.

- Sexual promiscuity and unawareness of responsible boundaries.

- Discouraged by the molesting parent from forming social contacts or dates with the opposite sex.

- Showing signs of discomfort sitting in chairs or playing games that require movement.

- Seeming older than their age—that is, a six-year-old seems like twelve.

- Displaying a "saddle walk" and having difficulty walking.

- Showing indication of warning genital symptoms; vaginal or anal bleeding; torn, stained, or bloody underclothes; pain or itching in the genital area; body odors in offensive proportion.[11]

In any classroom of twenty children, there are at least three sexual abuse victims.[12]

You may find this information overwhelming and feel like you should mind your own business. A common response to pain is withdrawal: "I don't want to know about it." "That doesn't happen here." But *children are everyone's business!* If you know of a child who displays these profiles, *you may be the only chance that child has!*

A few years ago in Atlanta, a TV and radio ad with lyrics by Tim McCabe carried this message:

> **You can see it in her eyes, you can tell there's something wrong and a part of you has to stop and ask, "Child, what's been going on?" He's a rough and tumble kid but there's more than meets the eye.**
>
> **There's a problem here and the truth, it seems, may be covered by a lie. It's okay to tell, there may be no one else who understands the problem. It's okay to tell, they're reaching out . . . can you stop and help them?**
>
> **A life could be in your hands, and if you really wish them well . . . then it's okay to tell.**

Four other potentially useful profiles follow:

Profile of suicidal behavior

- Social withdrawal and isolation.
- Giving away of prized possessions.
- Statements alluding to suicide (take every comment seriously, even if it comes as a joke).
- Actual threats of suicide or talking about ways to commit suicide.
- Hopelessness.
- Depression.
- Alcohol and other drug abuse.

- Intentional reckless behaviors, e.g., driving on wrong side of road or driving at high rates of speed.
- Loss of care/concern for personal hygiene.
- A sudden unexplainable "getting things in order," or "getting things out of order."[13]

Profile of teenage alcohol or other drug abuse

- Changes in appetite.
- Decreased ability to concentrate, sudden drop in grades.
- Excessive feelings of boredom.
- Changes in physical activity.
- Hypersensitive to words and actions of others.
- General irritability.
- Lies and steals.
- Misdirected anger; difficulty handling feelings.
- Difficulty handling stressful situations.
- Skipping school (especially Fridays and Mondays, or before and/or after holidays).
- Chronic illness, fatigue.
- Deterioration of personal appearance.
- Sudden disregard for family and school rules.
- Secretiveness, locking doors.
- Outbursts of inappropriate laughter.
- Unexplained bruises.
- Excessive coughs and colds.
- New friends who are rarely introduced to family.
- Mysterious phone calls.
- Increased tardiness at school.
- Suddenly short attention span and incoherent speech patterns.

- Runny nose with constant jaw movement and physically manifested nervousness.
- Dilated pupils of the eye or noticeably constricted. (Depends on whether amphetamines or barbiturates are being used.)
- Appearance of drug language in conversations.
- Redness and swollen eyes with accompanying erratic movement, rapid or slow.
- Slurring of words and unfinished sentences.
- Paranoia.[14]

Profile of abusive or neglectful parents

- They are isolated from family supports, such as groups.
- They consistently fail to keep appointments, discourage social contact, rarely or never participate in school activities.
- They seem to trust no one.
- They are reluctant to give information about the child's injuries or condition. They are unable to explain the injuries, or they give far-fetched explanations.
- They respond inappropriately to the child's condition, either by overreacting, or seeming hostile and antagonistic when questioned; or they underreact, showing little concern or awareness, and seem more occupied with their own problems than those of the child.
- They refuse to consent to diagnostic exams of the child.
- They delay or fail to take the child for medical care—for routine checkups or for treatment of injury or illness. Or they may choose a different doctor or hospital each time.
- They have unrealistic expectations of the child, expecting or demanding behavior that is beyond the child's years or ability.
- They believe in harsh punishment.
- They are overcritical.
- They seldom touch or look at the child.
- They ignore the child's crying or react with impatience.

- They keep the child confined, perhaps in a crib or playpen, for very long periods of time.
- They seem to lack understanding of the child's physical and emotional needs.
- They are hard to locate.
- They may be misusing alcohol or other drugs.
- They appear to lack control or fear that they may lose control.
- Their behavior may generally be irrational; they may seem incapable of child-rearing, and may seem to be cruel and sadistic.[15]

Profile of an abused spouse

- Is socially isolated and withdrawn. Avoids contact.
- Considers marriage a prison. The abused spouse may talk in extremes about it, as though it were a perfect marriage or a "Dante's" hell.
- Exhibits poor/low impulse control: i.e., yells, screams, and throws things.
- May have been abused as a child or witnessed her parents' violent relationship.
- Has low self-esteem. May feel the abuse is justified, that it is her fault.
- May be depressed and suicidal.
- Tends to be angry and fearful at the same time.
- Often denies the seriousness of the problem.
- Is usually codependent and will return to the relationship without treatment.
- Is usually dependent financially on spouse with little means of being self-supporting.
- May be apathetic: low motivation to do anything.
- May abuse alcohol, street drugs, and prescriptive medications.
- May have nervous habits and poor hygiene.
- Talks negatively about self and life in general.

- Wears sunglasses to hide blackened eyes, long-sleeved shirts to cover bruises. Other physical signs include swollen lips and broken teeth, scratch marks, and contusions.

These profiles are provided so that you can take vital steps in reporting any suspected family violence. No two victims or abusers are alike, and they do not display every indicator listed in these profiles. But they do display several of the indicators, if you're paying attention. We have a social responsibility to see that children are protected. By law, you cannot be prosecuted for reporting child abuse in good faith.[16] So get involved; your help is needed in stopping family violence.

IF YOU THINK A CHILD IS BEING ABUSED AT SCHOOL

Talk to your child or the parents of the children involved. Let your child know that you're interested and concerned, that you believe him. Listen without interrupting and don't overreact. Overreacting will cause the child to clam up or tell less than the truth, and you'll lose valuable information. Explain to your child that you will make certain that the situation will improve.

If there are any visible injuries, take photographs and get your child to a doctor at once. If possible, take color photographs. Do this calmly and without blame or angry statements about the teacher involved; the child is already scared and hurt. Explain your actions; tell the child that taking pictures will help provide proof so that the violence will not be repeated and that medical attention is necessary to care for the injury.

Contact the school authorities, including the teacher involved and the school principal. Ask the teacher to explain what happened. Listen carefully. Usually the teacher will talk with you and give his or her side of the story. Be calm and don't get involved in an argument. Stay with your point that physical punishment is unacceptable to you and that you do not like what happened.

If the teacher is willing, you may want to set up a meeting involving the principal, teacher, yourself, and the child for apologies and a commitment not to use physical punishment again. Doing this will give the child some relief about returning to school and not having to face the teacher alone. It also will provide the opportunity to discuss and resolve the child's behavior that was unacceptable to the teacher.

If this meeting with the teacher is unsatisfactory, call other parents of children in your child's class to see if any of their children witnessed the abuse.

Until the issue is resolved, have your child transferred to another class with a different teacher. Meet with the new teacher and establish rapport. If your child has had difficulty with acceptable classroom behavior, this is a good time to discuss such issues and how best to handle them.

If the abuse was severe, contact the authorities immediately. Contact the National Coalition to Abolish Corporal Punishment in Schools (1-614-898-0170) and contact an attorney for advice on your local state laws. If you can't afford an attorney, contact the American Civil Liberties Union (ACLU), which usually is located in the largest city in the state.

Cases of teachers physically abusing students are rare. Most have chosen their profession because of a strong sense of idealism and dedication to children. Your child will gain the most from being one corner of the education triangle—parents, teacher, student. When all three work as a team, rather than as antagonists, the child wins.

Those few teachers who abuse children may respond to intervention and become better teachers. Remember that they, too, may simply be repeating what they learned from their teachers and parents as a child. You can help introduce effective alternative forms of discipline that actually will make the teacher's job easier.

IF YOU WITNESS FAMILY VIOLENCE IN A PUBLIC PLACE

This is a tough problem. Who hasn't been in a grocery store and seen a child shaken or smacked by an angry, stressed parent? I witnessed one incident at Noah's Ark, a family restaurant west of St. Louis, Missouri. The restaurant is built in the shape of an ark and has animal forms everywhere, inside and outside.

Sitting adjacent to our table were a mother and her child, a little girl around the age of five. The mother's voice became louder with each "Shut up." And, of course, the child's demands became louder with each "Shut up." (I don't know when we're going to learn as parents that we get back what we give to our children. If we yell, they yell; if we hit, they hit; if we're angry, they're angry.)

Finally, this frustrated mother slapped the little girl across the face with a loud pop. A deafening silence followed. I saw the hurt, sad eyes of the little girl and then heard the intense wailing.

I watched the other diners keep their eyes glued on the food in front of them. The social group witnessing this incident didn't want to notice, didn't want to see. I felt helpless, angry, and more resolved than ever to learn how to handle that kind of scene when I next encountered it. When people lose their tempers in public, they are out of control and can be extremely hostile and defensive. That is not the time to lecture them. It is a time to provide social restraints and supportive peer pressure.

If you see a mother losing it with her children in a supermarket, you might say something to her in a compassionate way. "Boy, this reminds me of home. I have three kids myself and know how demanding they can be. Is there anything I can do to help?" This kind of contact is an intervention, an interruption of the crisis. It will act as a calming technique.

If the person is receptive to your friendly intervention, take time to listen. She or he may need to ventilate feelings, or she simply may thank you and resume shopping. But your intervention will not be forgotten. It serves as a reminder to this mother that society is watching and caring, that we are practicing a new level of thinking and being with our children.

If the person is hostile to your friendly intervention, back off and continue to watch at a distance. The intervention will still be working, as it has made the person aware that people are noticing. In rare cases in which the abuse may become violent, report the abuse by calling the police from the nearest public phone. Give descriptions and, if possible, a license plate number and the make of the car. Collect witnesses' names.

If you're in a large crowd and choose not to intervene, you can call other people's attention to what's happening. We are all very sensitive to one another. We know when someone is looking at us. We also interpret their intentions by body language—especially facial language. An abuser in a public place will feel the stares of a crowd quickly and, in most cases, will stop the abuse. Again, this intervention will not be forgotten. It may not cure or stop the private violence immediately, but it will be remembered and may eventually contribute to the person's recovery.

HOW TO PROTECT CHILDREN FROM ABUSE IN DAY-CARE SETTINGS

Anyone who followed the tragic story of the McMartin case, the longest, most expensive trial in United States history, is aware of the possible abuse that can occur in child-care facilities.[17] The alleged abuse occurred at the McMartin Preschool in Manhattan Beach, California, in 1983. A parent reported that her two-and-a-half-year-old son had been sodomized while the caregiver stuck the boy's head in a toilet, made him ride naked on a horse, and tormented him with an air tube. Though this woman's early accusations were insubstantial, by 1984 investigators concluded in a follow-up report that 369 of 400 children interviewed had been abused.[18] While the McMartin Preschool staff was acquitted, it is unlikely that 369 children had lied.

Reports of all types of child abuse and neglect in child-care facilities are becoming more common. Parents need to obtain adequate information about preventing and reporting instances of abuse.

Ten suggestions for parents' protecting their children while in other's care include:

1. Talk daily with your child. Talk about his or her activities. Ask for details. Do this without alarming your child. Be careful not to probe or prompt the child's answers. Good communication is the basis for good parenting.

2. Take time to listen closely when your child is talking. Remember, children do not speak directly about abuse at first; they will need your patience and gentle encouragement to talk.

3. Establish communication and an ongoing relationship with your child's caregiver(s). Get to know your child's caregivers and all other personnel within the child-care arrangement and facilities. Talk with them regularly about your child's care and behavior.

4. Make unannounced visits to observe your child's normal environment. Note the caregiver-to-child ratio, cleanliness, safety features, and time use. Watch for private, out-of-view places that children are sent for naps or time-out. Observe the personnel. Listen to their conversations. Do they care for and about children, or are they just putting in time?

5. Find out from your child's point of view what the rules are. Ask your child what happens when rules are broken.

6. Observe your child's play at home. Often children will act out situations to which they have been exposed. Have them draw a picture of the day at the center. Pay attention to any unusual themes and drawings of genitalia or abusive scenes. Question them about the drawing or their play; let them talk.

7. If your child has physical injuries, question how they happened. Note any sudden change in your child's emotional reaction or behavior while talking with him or her. In situations of sexual molestation, the child's behavior may be the only indicator.

8. Question the situation when the nature or extent of the injuries are not consistent with the explanation of what happened. A young boy was playing in a hayloft with three other companions. Two of the older boys became abusive and held a "hanging." They made the two younger boys stand on hay bales with their hands tied behind their backs, slipped nooses around their necks, and kicked the hay bales from under them. Somehow the young boys lived to tell about it.

I was one of those boys. I went home with rope burn marks on my neck. My sister, with whom I was staying at the time, asked me what had happened. I made up a story about a cat scratching my neck. My sister observed that the nature of my injury did not match the explanation given. Those older boys were in a lot of trouble.

9. Always maintain open communication. Establish a trusting relationship with your child. If you feel that your child has been abused, it isn't enough to remove her or him to another child-care center. You will leave other children at jeopardy if you don't report the abuse. Child abuse is a crime. Reporting it will help stop it. It also will get your family the help it needs to recover from the abuse. You must report the abuse to the local authorities.

IF YOU ARE AN ADULT SURVIVOR OF CHILD ABUSE

You may not recognize that you're an adult survivor of child abuse. Many people who were abused as children do, but others think that what they experienced was normal. Therefore, they repeat it with their own families. It's all they know to do. They may even be so stubborn about this that any new information about nonviolence is met with strong resistance and the feeling of being less of a man (or woman).

Here are some typical statements made by adult survivors of child abuse:

> "My father beat the daylights out of me several times, but I deserved it. And my boy gets the same thing when he deserves it!"

> "My mother used a hickory switch on my legs when I needed it!"

> "Why, yes, my father used his belt on many occasions; but I never was whipped that I didn't ask for it. I got what I asked for, and so do my kids!"

> "When my mother spanked me, I would yell with every blow, 'Ha, that didn't hurt!' She would just hit me harder until I would finally break down and cry. She wouldn't stop until I was humbled. I knew someday I would get her back!"

> "My parents didn't abuse me. They'd spank me and slap me around if I got out of line. But it taught me to toe the line. Now, my kids do the same. I don't take nothin' off them. They step out of line, I let them have it."

Adult survivors of child abuse (ASCA) live with tough memories of the past. Many suffer what the mental health profession calls post-traumatic stress disorder, or PTSD. The *DSM-III-R* defines PTSD as the development of characteristic symptoms following a psychologically distressing event that is outside the range of usual human experience. Victims generally experience intense fear and feelings of helplessness.[19]

One way survivors deal with the trauma of child abuse is to re-live it in their dreams and memories. It's like a shadow—it's always there reminding them of the past. Another way survivors deal with having been abused is to avoid anything associated with the trauma. War veterans will avoid war movies about their experience and protest that it is impossible for a movie to capture what it was really like. Adult survivors of child abuse will withdraw and feel estranged from others, just as they did as children. An intense response to being abused as a child is increased arousal—as indicated by insomnia, loss of concentration, and general irritability.

Not all adult survivors of child abuse suffer from PTSD. Depending on the degree of abuse, the following characteristics may apply:

- You are extremely self-critical;
- You are unaware of what being normal means;
- You accept violence as a way of life;
- You are wary of relationships, social contacts, and events;
- You are chronically ill;
- You simultaneously are chronically depressed and agitated;
- You are angry and distrustful toward authority figures;
- You are likely to feel guilty if things are going well;
- You are willing to martyr yourself in relation to others;
- You are feeling trapped in your marriage;
- You discipline your kids the same way you were disciplined;
- You are permissive with your kids so they don't experience what you did;
- You are critical and judgmental of others;
- You are extremely vengeful, always quick to retaliate;
- You are prone to yelling, screaming, cursing;
- You are surprised when people get so upset over your angry outbursts;
- Your marriage is unstable;
- You are threatened by criticism;
- You are fearful of success and bitter over failures;
- You are inclined to think that life owes you something but are not sure what;
- You are prone to abuse alcohol and other drugs; and/or
- You are fearful and paranoid.

If you're an adult survivor of child abuse and sick and tired of being sick and tired, here's what to do to get into recovery:

Talk about what happened. Talking about traumatic events is the first step in healing. In *The Courage to Heal*, a guide for survivors of child sexual abuse, Ellen Bass and Laura Davis write about why telling is transforming:

- You move through the shame and secrecy that keeps you isolated.
- You move through denial and acknowledge the truth of your abuse.
- You make it possible to get understanding and help.
- You get more in touch with your feelings.
- You get a chance to see your experience (and yourself) through the compassionate eyes of a supporter.
- You make space in relationships for the kind of intimacy that comes from honesty.
- You establish yourself as a person in the present who is dealing with the abuse in her past.
- You join a courageous community of women [or men] who are no longer willing to suffer in silence.
- You help end child sexual abuse by breaking the silence in which it thrives.
- You become a model for other survivors.
- You eventually feel proud and strong.[20]

Choose someone you trust with your confidences. Even people who are socially isolated usually have one or two people in their lives who will listen. Tell them about the experiences that are keeping you locked away from society and stuck in your loneliness. Telling someone else will be the key to a lock that needs to be opened.

Seek professional help and recapitulate. The longer you avoid looking at your pain, the longer the pain will last. *Catharsis*, a word for talking through and acting out, is often the breakthrough that is needed.

You will want to do this with a therapist trained in treating family violence.

Go in stages and relive the experience at your own pace. A sensitive therapist can guide this process at a pace for you to work through and break the cycle of violence in your life. In *The Teachings of Don Juan* by Carlos Castaneda, Don Juan called this process "recapitulation," in which the individual would place himself on a chair inside a box and talk about a past experience. By doing this, all of the unfinished feelings and energies surrounding the event could be dealt with as an adult and finally could be completed. As a child, you were overwhelmed and unable to deal with the emotional terror of your experience. As an adult, you can deal with it and stop it from controlling your life.

Forgive your parents. It's imprisoning to live life with a grudge against anyone, especially your parents. Vindictive fantasies are a waste of time, and judgmental feelings eat a hole in your stomach and accomplish nothing productive for you or the objects of your anger. Forgiveness is not an act that excuses the abuse or crime. It is an act that *releases you from the abuser*. It is an opportunity to release your life to a new future!

It is also a process of understanding without condemnation and seeing with compassion. Only by accepting the entire truth about your parents can we establish a basis for true compassion and love for them.

Forgiving your parents or abusing guardian does not condone the way they treated you. Neither does it mean that you will reconcile with them and live happily ever after. But forgiveness is an act of freedom that carries more power than revenge, more love than hatred, more understanding than judgment. It frees you to get on with your life and become a better person, a better spouse, a better parent. You are free to learn from your parents' mistakes. The goal of each generation is to develop beyond the previous one. This forward progression is blocked when you're unable to forgive.

Forgiveness will not come easily, but it will be easier than you expect. After you have completed the first two steps described above—telling and recapitulation—forgiveness will follow naturally.

Work on your own parenting skills; educate yourself. This is critical to stopping the learned cycle of violence. Remember, your parents were repeating what they had learned and you will repeat what you learned. To break the cycle of family violence, you must learn new skills and ways of parenting.

Read books. Read as many parenting books and child development materials as you can. Chapter 4 of this book offers tips on effective parenting. Start, but don't stop, there! The more information you learn, the better parent you will become.

Many parents do not understand the age-level stages of development of their children. A mother sat in my office angrily stating, "My two-year-old says no to everything I say or do. She wants her own way and plays by herself a lot. Her temper tantrums are out of control. What's wrong with her, anyway?"

It's simple—two-year-old children dislike taking orders, want their own way, and like to play alone. Temper tantrums, a newly discovered way of expression for them, are normal for this age. It will pass—unless the parent takes it on, and then two temper tantrums may be the end result!

Participate in parenting workshops. Take every opportunity to get training as a parent. Workshops provide three important opportunities for improving your skills as a parent. You receive the latest information on parent-child relations that work. You meet with other parents and form a supportive network. And, most important, you are focusing on trying to be an effective parent.

Work on your marriage. Good marriages produce good parents. Good parents produce healthy children. Children are like mirrors. To see the state of a marriage, all we have to do is look in the mirrors. Children in a crumbling marriage can display chaos and extreme behavior that attempts to control the dissolving environment that once was safe and secure. Show me an angry child, and I'll show you an angry parent. Show me a depressed child, and I'll show you a depressed or abusive parent.

It has been playfully noted in our culture that pets often display the personality of their owners, even to similarities in appearance. I do know that children display the personality of their parents. The best gift parents can give a child, then, is a good marriage. Chapter 4, which has a section on marriage skills, is a good place to start. But do more than read about how to make your marriage work; seek help with a marriage therapist if things are rough and you haven't been able to stop the conflict or resolve it. Get involved in marriage enrichment programs and prioritize your relationship with the time, energy, and attention required.

Emphasizing marriage undoubtedly will create discomfort to single parents. The truth is, divorce scars children. But it's a matter of degree—the angrier, more hostile divorces are the hardest on the children. Couples who can divorce without centering the children in a loyalty conflict and power struggle will have the best results. Divorce mediation is advised, wherein the family therapist will direct negotiations with the child's best interests as the priority.

Single parenting is tough! The stress placed on two parents is tough enough; but when there is only one primary parent, the risks of abuse increase. Single parents need to reach out and utilize as many community resources as possible. Organizations like Parents Without Partners and Big Brothers help with parenting and provide possibilities for support groups and shared baby-sitting co-ops.

Children need relief from adults, too, just as adults do from children. Children in a stable marriage require time alone and time away. Single parents sometimes become overprotective and possessive. When the child also learns to be protective and possessive, the parent-child relationship can become strained. The more support and help a single parent gets, the better.

It's important to know that children fare better if a severely dysfunctional marriage ends in divorce. Divorce can be one of the best things that ever happens to your children. Certainly, in the case of spouse abuse, substance abuse, and/or child abuse, the children are not safe. The cessation of such a marriage is often the preferred and necessary action to stop the abuse. Also, children will learn a very important lesson: if your husband or spouse abuses you or your children, you leave! You don't stay and put up with it.

Stop all abuse of alcohol and other drugs. Alcohol and other drugs are ways of life for many adult survivors of child abuse. It doesn't matter where you learned it. What matters is that you stop using and get into recovery. Drug abuse keeps you depressed. It eventually leads to impotence and, finally, death. It is a slow form of suicide. It keeps you in a vicious circle that is spiraling self-destruction. What helps you escape for short periods of time keeps you imprisoned long-term. Alcohol and other drugs anesthetize pain. Their use becomes a way of forgetting the pain or creating a state of being called, by Martin Heidegger in *Being and Time*, a "forgetfulness of being."[21]

When beginning recovery, you feel like you're going crazy. This is because you're no longer anesthetized in a "state of forgetfulness of being." Suddenly you're back to being in the moment, aware of the hardness of life. The truth is, however, that when in recovery, you begin to go sane. You've been crazy. That was easy. The hard part is being sane! Hang on; it's a rough ride till the new horse is trained.

Being in recovery is making a statement for renewal and for changing old patterns. It is a great gift to yourself, your spouse, and your children. It will require a lot of effort on your part. Individual and group therapy require a concentration of your time and resources. You will need to attend AA meetings or Narcotics Anonymous (NA) or both. I usually recommend two meetings a week with the commitment that if you fall off the wagon, you attend ninety AA meetings in ninety days! Then, if you fall off the wagon during those ninety days, the next step is to check in to an inpatient treatment program.

One common excuse given for avoiding treatment for substance abuse is lack of money. I advise the therapists I train not to give any slack at all to clients addicted to alcohol and/or other drugs. I also advise having them pay for ten sessions in advance, which can be very expensive. The reason for this is to test their commitment to recovery and see if they're willing to shift the money usually spent for the addiction to treatment. One cocaine addict I worked with resisted inpatient treatment because it cost close to twelve thousand dollars. Yet he fell off the wagon and borrowed six thousand dollars to continue his crack run. It's all in how you're going to prioritize your life. You have to decide what you're going to invest in—your life and your children, or your addiction.

Put away the paddle forever! You have to decide to be in recovery if the violence is to stop—or someone has to decide for you. It is better for you and your family to do this. Outside intervention may lead to separation from your loved ones.

Most batterers begin recovery by seeking professional help. Turn to the section earlier in this chapter, "If You Are Abusing Your Spouse or a Family Member," and review the steps given there. A typical treatment plan will involve two or three months of individual therapy and six to twelve months of group therapy. The number-one priority of the therapist is to stop the violence.

Only after this has been accomplished and you've been in sufficient individual treatment should conjoint therapy begin. Conjoint therapy includes your spouse and children. The treatment is a restructuring and reeducating process. You will be practicing new ways of thinking and being. Make a commitment to put away the abuse you experienced as a child—forever. It can be done, and it is the only hope for your children to be functional, healthy human beings who contribute to their family and society. They'll do this as the result of your contribution of recovery! Recovery is a contribution to your self, family, and society.

IF YOU ARE ELDERLY AND BEING ABUSED

On my seventieth birthday I said, "In my old age I need three things: good health, loads of money, and somebody who gives a damn." Seventeen years later, at eighty-seven, I stand by my list except I've changed the priorities: somebody who cares has moved to first place!
—Elizabeth S. Force, Ph.D.

By the year 1996, there will be 7.5 million Americans over eighty years of age. Almost 85 percent of the 25.5 million elders in America today suffer from at least one chronic disease, and an estimated 2 million elderly people need help with daily living activities.[22] This dependency provides the stressful setting in which elder abuse is most likely to occur.

The problem of elder abuse is increasing as Americans' life spans increase, with accompanying needs for caregiving. When one spouse can no longer care for the other, caregiving commonly becomes the responsibility of children and grandchildren. In family violence, roles are reversed and intergenerational transmission of violent behavior is repeated on the original abusers.

Many victims of elder abuse were at one time abusive toward their children.

Elders in poor health are very much like small children, helpless and defenseless. Much of elder abuse can and must be stopped by social intervention. The American public needs to become as involved in elder abuse as it is in child abuse, reporting any known abuse.

Elders' isolation is a primary reason why their abuse is problematic and not yet receiving much attention. Our elders are not involved in mandatory schools, employment, or social networks like children and young adults are. Often confined to the homes of their abusers and fearful of being sent to a rest home, elders are more reluctant to report abuse than any other victim of family violence. Reports indicate that only one in four known cases of elder abuse are reported by the victims themselves.

As many as six million elders are abused in the United States each year.[23]

Here are some of the reasons why victims of elder abuse do not report it to authorities:

- It is difficult to know to whom to report. No national hotline exists for elder abuse.

- Elders fear being institutionalized.

- Victims often blame themselves for their abusers' actions.

- Victims are ashamed and embarrassed to admit publicly that their own children or grandchildren are mistreating them.

- Their codependent love for the abuser is stronger than the abuse itself.

- They are more concerned about the well-being of their abusers than about their own safety and well-being.

- Abuse has been accepted as a way of living. They learned it as children, used it on their children, accept it from their adult children.

- Victims may be disabled and unable to make contact with the outside world.

- They are socially isolated. They have no teachers, employers, or social contacts to report the abuse for them. Families can hide elder abuse more easily than any other form of family violence.

The prototype of an abuser is a middle-aged female daughter or daughter-in-law who has just finished raising her own children and feels strapped with caring for another dependent member of the family. Mothers have an extremely difficult loyalty conflict in reporting their own daughters. (The typical victim of elder abuse is an older female residing in her daughter's home.)

If you are an elder and you're being abused, take the following steps:

Talk to someone other than the offender about the abuse. You will need an advocate, someone to stand with you against any further abuse. Choose someone whom you trust and who is not involved in the abuse. State clearly that you want to avoid being placed in a nursing home as a solution to the abuse. Try to procure counseling for your abuser and yourself with a therapist who will closely monitor the cessation of abuse. Once abuse is made public and therapeutic intervention is made, in most cases, the offender will stop the abuse.

Leave if the abuse is severe and if you are able. If you are unable to leave the scene of abuse, dial 911 and ask for the police. You also can call the National Council on Aging or one of the referral numbers in appendix A in this book for advice on what to do in your geographical area. Remember, violent behavior does not get better without helpful intervention. It gets worse. The older you become, the more vulnerable you will be and the less able to do something about the abuse. Do everything you can, now, to get help. *Don't put up with being abused.*

If you are able to leave, follow those steps described in the first section of this chapter that apply to you. If you don't have a safe, predetermined place to go, some shelters for battered women and other social agencies offer help to grandmothers and mothers. You have protection under the Family Violence Act, which requires the police to intervene if you're being severely assaulted.

Unfortunately, like child abuse used to be, elder abuse often is ignored. Not enough is being done to stop elder abuse—we are decades behind! State laws that mandate reporting of elder abuse are difficult to enforce. Often elder abuse is ignored by family, friends, and the community.

When a case of elder abuse is reported, authorities' options are limited. If it is necessary to remove the elder from the abusing home, most likely he or she is moved to a nursing home. Most victims of elder abuse are more willing to stay in their violent environment than be institutionalized. Social services for elder abuse are about twenty to thirty years behind the development of services for other victims of family violence. It's going to take public awareness and mass attention to play "catch up." Yesterday is not soon enough to deal with this problem.

One of the better options is to get the offending caregiver into treatment and contracted for stopping the violence. The hard part is getting them into treatment. Don't give up and don't give in; call for help. Court-ordered treatment can be as effective as voluntary treatment. If you're being abused, call today!

IF YOU ARE A VIETNAM VETERAN

Several years ago, I found myself standing before the reflective black marble wall of the Vietnam Memorial in Washington, D.C., staring at the name of a friend on that wall of haunting memories and nightmares. I rediscovered a deep cistern of bitter tears surfacing after twenty years of not talking about it, smothering and trying to ignore my pain. I looked around and found comfort in the presence of other weeping men and women. A colleague of mine, himself a Vietnam veteran, stood before the wall with his son one day, and his little boy said, "Everyone here has eyes like yours, Dad!"

People ask why our society is so violent. We don't seem to understand the nature of violence. It is as though some outside entity invades our social order and we look for causes outside ourselves. Yet our entire history contains episodic violence. Since early humans' development of boundaries, wars and threats of war have erupted to protect or conquer.

The nature of violence bears repeating in this brief section on Vietnam veterans. It applies to all war veterans, but Vietnam is a pervasive American memory of violence. Often-hostile reception of Vietnam vets compounded postwar recovery.

Breakdown is a descriptive word for the road back from Vietnam. Post-traumatic stress disorder (PTSD) is the clinical label for this road back from hell. War is the craziest action of humankind! It teaches and practices mental illness. Then, when the war is over and the veteran returns home, he or she suddenly is expected to be mentally healthy. The returning Vietnam veteran asked, "Where the hell do I fit in?"

Full of stories and the need to tell them, returning Vietnam vets discovered that *no one wanted to listen.* Vets didn't talk to anyone about the experiences that had eaten a hole in their souls. I recall vividly the experience of being in the Gulf of Tonkin off the coast of Vietnam one month and the next month being on a college campus in the Midwest, where students were carrying black coffins and banners of protest. Instead of being able or willing to talk about my experience, I kept it inside.

With no one listening, Vietnam vets withdrew into silent observance of the anger and disdain of social complaints. It was confusing. Our culture had trained them to do what they did. They were serving our country. Bitterness was deepened by unemployment.

Vietnam had turned our world upside down and when we stepped back on our own land, it was chaotic and disoriented. Crazy was still normal to us.

Many Vietnam vets never readjusted. Some became hermits, living in the woods or in small, isolated communities. Some turned, or returned, to alcohol and other drugs to experience one of the only means of "forgetfulness of being" available to them in Vietnam. Still others tried and failed at several marriages while unable to hold down a steady job due to lost motivation and flarebacks of anger and rage.

Reentry requires reeducation. What had been normal became abnormal. An important beginning is to learn about violence. The following characteristics of violence are applicable to family violence as well as to the war experience of veterans. Violence has no clearly definable boundaries.

Characteristics of violence:

1. Violence repeats itself. It creates its own vicious cycle. Even in defeat, a person or nation does not forget. Monuments and memorials are constructed on both sides of victory and defeat. Walls are constructed to keep people in and keep people out. Cold wars are born out of people's fears that what happened once can happen again. The dynamics of family violence are similar.

   Parent-child relationships become entrenched in I'll-show-you or I'll-get-you-back attitudes. Walls are constructed to keep children in and keep parents out.

2. It's always justified by the users and abusers. Reasons are created for the violence: "I hit her because she asked for it!" "My kid smart-mouthed me one too many times. I had to teach him a lesson."

3. Violence is reciprocal. It establishes a polarity. Each side of the action establishes that the other side is evil and worthy of

being destroyed. When little boys grow up and become trained machines of national defense, reciprocity is known as patriotism and the make-believe fantasies become real.

4. There is no difference in violence on either side of the conflict. Violence is violence. Whether it was the U.S. Calvary at Wounded Knee or the Indian nations at Custer's Last Stand, the violence was all the same. There's no such thing as good violence versus bad violence. I have heard many Vietnam veterans say that the Vietcong were ruthless, but in fact, so were we. Many of the victims of PTSD suffer from the memories of their own violent actions in Vietnam.

Vietnam veterans suffering from PTSD are more reactive than responsive in relationships. Quick to react, to defend, or attack. In Vietnam they had to trust the troops around them. Now they don't have to trust anyone and often lash out at friends and family in angry outbursts, emotional internal monologues and violence.

As soldiers, they tended to carry on the culturally expected roles of bravery and valor in battle, when actually, they were young boys scared out of their wits in a hostile environment. The average age of the American soldier in Vietnam was 18.5. They made retreats into alcohol and other drug abuse, enemy flag burning, and revelry in attempts to regain a sense of belonging.

One very important fact needs to be realized by men and women suffering from PTSD and/or recurring violence or thoughts of violence: the Vietnam experience is seldom the sole cause of PTSD or family violence. Much of current dysfunction has its roots in childhood. Granted, Vietnam did provide the kind of dysfunctional setting that precipitates emotional stress and breakdown.

Our first family unit is called the family of origin. Whether it was a functional or dysfunctional family, the children developed a sense of belonging. If your parents were violent with you, your memories may be of not belonging; but children do everything they can to belong—even in chaos. Abused children, for example, often will go to the abusing parent for the most attention. To a child, negative attention is better than no attention at all. By the time of adolescence and teenage years, the child figures out that his or her violent home is not a very secure place of belonging.

Therefore, a search begins for a new place of belonging. Distance is created from the family of origin. Peers become the focus of relationships and birds of a feather flock together. Abused kids find one another and attempt to build, through substance abuse, rebellion, promiscuity, and other antisocial behaviors, a sense of belonging.

Just like the child figuring out a place of belonging in a dysfunctional family, the Vietnam vet figured out quickly a place of belonging in the chaos of Vietnam. In fact, Vietnam's confused boundaries in hostile territory were amplifications of earlier family violence for a lot of the vets.

One veteran said, "It was similar to but better than my original family. In the jungle you had to depend on each other. You were a close-knit small family with your life in each other's hands. You became close without knowing any first names."

In scanning Vietnam publications, like *Vietnam* magazine, this sense of family is evident in article titles and their content. For example, one title reads: "General Lewis W. Walt—'Uncle Lew' to his Marines—was the stuff of which legends are made."[24]

With PTSD, the Vietnam vet becomes obsessed with memories of this dysfunctional place of belonging because it was the family of choice he never had as a child. He remembers his buddies with a fixed notion of loyalty and good feelings. To have had brothers you could rely on in the violent environment of Vietnam provided a welcome sense of belonging. Everyone needs to feel welcome and appreciated, safe and secure, wanted and loved.

Anyone suffering from PTSD struggles with:

- intrusive thoughts and flashbacks;

- insomnia and recurring nightmares;

- social isolation and paranoia;

- believing that no one can understand;

- psychic numbing, avoiding emotions for fear of losing control;

- depression and suicidal thoughts;

- low self-esteem and fear of success;

- angry outbursts and antisocial behavior;

- guilt for surviving;

- self-sabotaging in relationships and career;

- anxiety attacks or nervousness;

- inability to achieve intimacy and normal family life;

- denial—may deny having any damage from Vietnam experience;

- substance abuse and denial; and

- distrust of anyone with authority.

If you're a Vietnam veteran suffering from violent outbursts and PTSD, *talk to someone about it*.

In *The Teachings of Don Juan*, Carlos Castaneda is taught the art of recapitulation by the old Yaqui Indian sorcerer, Don Juan. Recapitulation is a catharsis, a talking out and working through lingering energies left over from traumatic events in the warrior's life. The warrior was seated in a box and encouraged to talk about major life crises in his past that still were affecting his life. He would stay in the box until he was finished with the haunting energies of the past. Once free, he would return to his tribe, renewed.

The natural healing process of any trauma is begun in the telling of stories about what was seen and experienced. In the telling of our stories, we find a way to:

1. communicate who we were;

2. talk about who we have become;

3. discover who we want to be;

4. understand our experiences and what we've learned; and

5. become responsible for the stories we're re-creating and living today.

When we begin to realize that we are responsible for creating memories, we begin to be more careful about designing the rest of our lives. We can design our lives to be in dysfunctional memories of the past or to be functional memories of the present that we're creating. Instead of the memory shaping you, you can shape the memories into a more useful purpose in your life.

In the evening, for example, I can choose to remember the horror of Vietnam, or I can spend quality time with my six-year-old son, embracing him with gentleness and affirming love. Feeling his tiny hand pat me on the head and hearing his little boy voice say, "I love you, Daddy; you're the bestest daddy in the whole wide world," is a memory far more functional than anything I can recall from Vietnam. How we spend our time in memories is our responsibility and choice!

Memories don't happen to us. We happen to them. We're not victims of memories; we're deciders of memories. The more we tell our stories out loud, the less priority we will give them inside. You see, if we don't tell our stories in the community, then we tell them inside to ourselves—over and over—and they become an obsession. Stories have to be told in the community in order to take away their secretive power in our lives.

Find someone who will listen—a friend, a pastor, a counselor. Don't choose another Vietnam vet who is as angry and mired in his memories as you are. That would be like putting behavioral problem children together and expecting them to figure out better ways of behaving. All they would do is reinforce the unacceptable behaviors. Do you want to get angrier than you already are about Vietnam? Join a group of Vietnam vets who are committed to substance abuse and burning Vietcong flags around campfires, men who tell war horror stories and are consumed by bitterness. Do you want to get better instead of bitter about your war experience? Read on.

Seek professional help. Don't try to fix yourself. *You can't do it alone.* The experience of Vietnam is too overwhelming. Search for a therapist you trust. You may feel better with a therapist who is a Vietnam veteran. Or perhaps you'd prefer one who has not been in the service. You decide and then make contact. Professional intervention and care can help you create a new way of life, a new way of being.

I recommend licensed, private-practice psychotherapists and marriage and family therapists who provide the sanctuary of personal, one-to-one attention and small-group settings. You may want to work through the Veteran's Administration (VA) if you're disabled. However, private practitioners have a difficult time becoming fee providers through the VA, which creates a shortage of caregivers for Vietnam vets suffering from PTSD.

Seek a professional helper with a case load that will provide the opportunity for your treatment to be a priority. If you're suffering from substance abuse, depression, or any disability, make certain the therapist has a staff or consulting psychiatrist to carefully monitor any necessary medications during the course of your therapy.

Work on improving your marriage and upgrade your parenting skills. (See p. 101.)

Stop using all alcohol and other drugs. This bears repeating. Alcohol and other drugs create a state of "forgetfulness of being." Healing occurs when we are willing to remember and release old wounds. We have to be willing to be in a state of "wholeness of being." That means being willing to pay attention to the moment, to what is happening now. To be *awake*.

The past is a memory. It can happen now only if you choose it to be present. We are not victims of our minds. Our minds are like computers. We choose which disk to put in to call forth memory selection. We click the icons of Vietnam just like we click memories of old lovers and childhood experiences. They're only icons, and they don't have to be clicked onto your memory screen all the time. You can learn how to create new programs and input new functional memories. Neurolinguistic therapy is very effective in helping create and instill new thought patterns in a process known as "anchoring." Alcohol and other drugs, however, block this process and keep the computer rigged for the past. The present can be anesthetized into oblivion while we live in unpleasant memories that can trigger violence in present relationships.

If you're addicted to alcohol and other drugs, you will need some highly structured treatment that includes support groups like Alcoholics Anonymous (AA) and Narcotics Anonymous (NA). Your family should attend Al-Anon in conjunction with your treatment. If you want help, if you want to change, the *substance abuse has to go.*

Know that you're a lovable human being. Vietnam vets often display symptoms of low self-esteem and judgmental self-destructiveness. The war is over. There's a lovable little kid inside of you who deserves better than you're being. That's because you've never learned how to love yourself.

It's hard for victims of child abuse to grow up loving themselves. They have to learn how. Join a Vietnam vet support group that is committed to recovery or get into a group therapy setting where you can work on this growth with trained guidance.[25]

NOTES

1. R. Day, ed., *Plain Talk about Wife Abuse*, flyer, National Institute of Mental Health, Division of Scientific and Public Information, DHHS publication no. ADM 83-1265, 1983.

2. S. Forward, *Toxic Parents* (New York: Bantam Books, 1989), p. 73.

3. On February 15, 1990, the Associated Press carried the following headlines and news story: "Slain boy's torturer gets life in prison...mom who let it happen receives same sentence.... In sentencing, Circuit Judge Michael B. Getty said if he had let emotions dictate his actions, he would have given the two the death penalty for the 'vicious, brutally sadistic torture and murder of Lattie McGee.' The life sentences carry no possibility of parole."

4. A special thanks to my colleague David Reed, M.S.W., for his contribution to this section. He has twenty years' experience working with dysfunctional families and troubled adolescents.

5. Dr. Frank Walton on teenage suicide. Dr. Walton is past president of the North American Society of Adlerian Psychology.

6. Ibid.

7. This book is not intended to provide in-depth treatment plans and modalities. Every family therapist whom you contact will bring a uniquely specific training and theoretical approach to the problem. The important thing is that you contact a licensed marriage and family therapist and start treatment immediately.

8. M. E. Traicoff, "Family Interventions from Women's Shelters," in *Clinical Approaches to Family Violence* (Rockville, Md.: Aspen Publication, 1989), p. 109.

9. Georgia Department of Human Resources, forms 423, 425, and 428.

10. Family Counseling Service of Athens, Georgia, Teen Counseling Program brochure.

11. Jerry L. Brinegar, "Child Abuse and Neglect Workshop for Teachers" (Athens, Ga.: New Beginnings Marriage and Family Therapy, 1985).

12. Ruth Soukup, Sharon Wickner, and Joanne Corbett, *Three in Every Classroom* (Gonvick, Minn.: Richards, 1984), p. 3.

13. Frank Walton and Iris Bolton, *An Approach to Intervention* (Columbia, S.C.: Lexington Communications, 1986).

14. Family Counseling Service of Athens and J. L., Brinegar.

15. Georgia Department of Human Resources, form 423.

16. Channing L. Bete Company, *What Everyone Should Know about Child Abuse,* scriptographic booklet, Channing L. Bete, 1976, p. 12.

17. Margaret Carlson, "Six Years of Trial by Torture," *Time*, January 29, 1990, p. 26.

18. Ibid.

19. "Treatment of Adult Survivors of Childhood Abuse," *Diagnostic and Statistical Manual of Mental Disorders*, 3rd ed., revised (Washington, D.C.: American Psychiatric Association, 1987), pp. 247·48.

20. E. Bass and L. Davis, *The Courage to Heal* (New York: Harper and Row, 1988), p. 95.

21. M. Heidegger, *Being and Time* (New York: Harper and Row, 1962).

22. R. Bleiszner and J. M. Alley, "Family Caregiving for the Elderly: An Overview of Resources," *Family Relations, Journal of Applied Family and Child Studies* (January 1990), p. 97.

23. J. Saltman, *The Many Faces of Family Violence*, pamphlet, Center for Women Policy Studies and the House Select Committee on Aging Public Affairs, p. 9.

24. R. A. Lynn, "Uncle Lew," *Vietnam* magazine (Leesburg, Va., April 1990), p. 8.

25. Organizations like Point Man Ministries, a Christian Outreach for vets by vets of the Vietnam War in Wilkes-Barre, Pennsylvania, provide helpful information on workshops and support groups.

4

THE BREAKTHROUGH

MAKING MARRIAGE WORK

The Nature of Marriage

**One of the best gifts parents can give their children
is a healthy, functional marriage.**

If the goal of a healthy marriage isn't possible, divorce can be another
of the best gifts. By definition, a marriage is dysfunctional if it condones violence. If the abuser does not get into recovery, the marriage
will not get better. "Till death us do part" needs to be understood as
death occurring within the relationship as well as in life. Relationships
die, and divorce can be the best option for everyone involved, especially children.

A healthy, functional marriage is possible, but marriage is hard
work. Zen Buddhism has a saying: "After enlightenment, the laundry!"
For marriage it's: "After the honeymoon, the work!"

> **In every marriage more than two weeks old, there
> are grounds for divorce. The trick is to find, and
> continue to find, grounds for marriage.**
> **—Robert Anderson, *Double Solitaire***

It takes more strength and courage to maintain a marriage than it does
to break one up. Carl Whitaker says of marriage, "The greatest ordeal in
life is marriage. It is the central focus for enlightenment and the natural
therapeutic process in culture."[1] If this statement is true, marriage is a

healthy place to be. Goals of marriage include procreation, companionship, and belonging. Marriage usually begins with romantic blinders that block a total awareness of who the other person is and
maintains a high state of attraction to ensure procreation.

**The Talmud states it well: "Every goose is a
swan in the eyes of a lover!"**

Eventually the blinders come off. You wake up one morning, look
across the bed, and wonder, Who are you, and where did you come
from? The marriage is plunged into an identity crisis, and the task of
transformation from eros to companionate love begins. Children com-
plicate this setting with their needs and demands for attention. Until
the first child is born, the couple has more time to play, to focus on
mating frenzy, which is the culmination of the animal dance.

The Animal Dance

To achieve procreation, men and women experience something similar to an "animal dance."

Several years ago, I was fortunate to have an office with a splen-
did view of the mountains. Outside my office window was a dramatic
scene: plush, multicolored mountains, trees, and a large pasture split
by a small creek. A blended mix of cattle grazed outside in this pastoral
setting. One April afternoon, a young couple was sitting in my office
expressing frustration with their sex life. I was trying to listen carefully
to their words, but springtime was pulling my attention outside. In full
view behind this young couple were a bull and heifer mating.

The young man's words echoed in the room, "She doesn't turn
me on anymore."

"All he wants to do is stick it in and get it over with," she re-
torted.

I couldn't keep my mind on their conversation; too much was
happening outside and not enough was happening inside!

I watched the animal dance of that bull and heifer. It was exciting! It began with the heat of the heifer. Having been raised on a farm,
I knew that along with that seasonal heat comes a strong scent that is
carried by the soft, luring wind to the bull. The bull made his approach
from the far side of the pasture.

"You haven't heard a word we've said," the young wife complained. "You're sitting there looking out the window."

100

They both turned to see what I saw. By this time, the bull had nudged the heifer into position, but she kept coyly moving away. She would "bump and run," not standing still until the right moment arrived. The bull became more excited and impatient. Finally, the heifer stood her ground and the bull mounted her. The young couple were hypnotized by what they were seeing. The next day, they called in to report that they had spent the night making passionate love and thanked me for a great session. I credited the animal dance.

Marriage requires a maturing in sexuality. The animal dance changes. It is not a static experience in a vacuum that can be carried through life in its original packaging. Sexuality is fluid and responsive to the various stages of life and aging. No set rules explain how a couple should relate to each other sexually. A marriage that began with intercourse five to ten times a week can evolve to one with sex five times a year. And that relationship might be much richer, with priorities focusing on companionship and parenting more than on sexual intercourse.

Despite our cultural obsession with sex in advertising and the movies, sexuality involves far more than sexual intercourse itself. It involves our total beings, our identities in relationship to each other and the environment, and our roles as parents, teachers, neighbors, and friends.

The animal dance is just one part of this totality and is reserved in many species as the beginning of pair bonding. Many species pair with one mate for life. The animal dance is a luxury. It feels so good that it guarantees procreation of the species.

Giving birth to life is a sacred privilege. Yet it often brings the marriage to a state of breakdown. Babies change everything! Married life is never the same after the birth of the first child. Attention focused before on each other and genitalia becomes focused on diapers, sleep-disturbed nights, and incredibly delightful hours of bonding with your child. Wedding bells and honeymoons are replaced with child care and exhaustion. Both parents have to make major adjustments in their lifestyles.

Just because procreation is fulfilled is no reason for the dance to discontinue. Special efforts must be made by both mates to generate time and attention for each other. Following are some helpful suggestions and skills that will help strengthen and improve marital relationships.

Careful Mate Selection

There is nothing in human affairs so strange as the readiness of men, this side of senility, to pursue women, unless it be the readiness of women, this side of the grave, to be pursued.[2]

In this readiness, men and women pitch toward carelessness in the pursuit. Hormonal fulfillment in hurried desperation often ends in a terrible mess. Mate selection can be haphazard. It is not taught in high school or college; our society has left it to the family, which regenerates itself for better or for worse. Young people would benefit from education in the process of selecting a suitable mate.

Marriages are not made in heaven. Without careful mate selection, they can be made in hell. I've heard it said that women marry men hoping that they'll change and they don't, and men marry women hoping they'll never change and they do.

People who get married because of sparkling Hollywood passion usually end up very disappointed and bouncing from marriage to marriage in search of the prince or princess who's going to keep their Timex ticking forever. There's nothing wrong with sparkling passion; in fact, it's great! However, it needs to be tempered with thoughtful selection. In the animal kingdom, mate selection is often a long, painstaking dance of careful selection. It enables the female to choose with greater discrimination the mate who will be the father of her offspring. Human beings would do well to take note.

An ancient story tells about Nasrudin, who was in search of the perfect woman. He searched high and low, far and near, and found no one dear. In his old age, his friend asked him to explain why he had not found the perfect woman. Nasrudin replied, "Once I thought I had found her. She was beautiful beyond words and fun to be with. Though near perfect, she was not enough. Another time I found a woman who was intelligent and we had exciting conversations and enjoyed each other's company, but she was not as beautiful as the first woman. Still another woman I shall never forget. She was both beautiful and bright. She had the personality of all. She was perfect."

Nasrudin fell silent and his friend encouraged him on, "Go on, tell me, why didn't you marry her if she was the perfect woman?"

Nasrudin sadly replied, "Well, it didn't work out." He paused and shook his head. "It seems as though she were searching for the perfect man."[3]

The process of mate selection evolves through six stages, whether or not one is noticing the progression. In whirlwind romances, some stages are condensed drastically, which can lead to trouble.

Stage one of mate selection involves social events and settings that include work, church, school, dances, meetings—places where you are around other people. In stage one, many possibilities go unnoticed until something is said or something happens to get each other's attention.

Stage two is when you begin to pay attention to responses of attraction. You may be in a religious education class or PTA meeting and notice another person looking at you intensely—or maybe you are the one doing the looking. Glances connect. Interest is shown with smiles, eye contact, and conversations. It's still early in the selection process; this level of attention can be experienced with many individuals purely on a social level. Within the possibilities of mating, potential mates begin the process of narrowing choices based on attractiveness and initial responses. Some dating may occur at this level, but nothing steady or serious.

Stage three is the level that begins to require selective attention to responsive attraction. You start to narrow down the field of possibilities to a few potential mates. Dating becomes more selective, and you are more aware of emotions and thoughts. The third stage is usually brief, as you move quickly on the strongest set of feelings and responses. This can be dangerous and ill advised if you're following your heart and not your mind.

Stage three requires careful selection based on our assessment of what characteristics we want in a spouse and why, or else we simply repeat old data. It's extremely important for adult survivors of family violence to know that freedom of choice is possible, that we are not victims of emotions that happen to us. We are choosers of emotions, and we can change our mate selection process by being more aware while making more responsible choices.

Carl Jung talked about mate selection in terms of the conscious and unconscious mind. "The greater the area of unconsciousness, the less is marriage a matter of free choice, as is shown subjectively in the fatal compulsion one feels so acutely when one is in love"[4] "It is the strength of the bond to the parents that unconsciously influences the choice of husband or wife, either positively or negatively. Conscious love for either parent favors the choice of a like mate, while an unconscious tie (repressed unfinished business) makes the choice difficult and imposes characteristic modifications."[5] And "the one who is grounded on a positive relationship to the parents will find little or no difficulty in adjusting to his or her partner, while the other may be hindered by a deep-seated unconscious tie to the parents."[6]

The more in touch you are with your childhood and what it was like growing up in your family, the better enabled you will be to make a good selection of a mate. The more complete you are with your father and mother, the clearer you will be in what you're looking for in a mate. If your father was gentle, kind, and affectionate, search for a gentle, kind, and affectionate male. If he was an alcoholic, distant, and prone toward violent outbursts, search for a man who doesn't drink, is not afraid of intimacy, and is nonviolent.

Good marriages are made easier by the couple's own positive parenting experiences. But before blaming all of your problems on the past, know that:

**Regardless of your childhood, you are responsible
for your current choices and actions.**

If you had a bad childhood, you'll just have to work harder to have a good marriage. You can do it! You are responsible for whether or not you repeat your parents' mistakes. Your past does not happen to you now. It doesn't automatically repeat itself. You can choose a different path, a different way of being. If your father hit your mother, declare your disapproval and seek nonviolent resolution of conflict. Be the generation that learns a better way.

Stage four is narrowing the field down to the "main squeeze." You make a choice to temporarily stop other dating and you begin some serious dating with one person. Sexual interest or activity increases throughout stages one through three, and now it's front and center. Once you decide how to handle this (some people wait, others don't), you either move to the commitment stage or return to stage one and start the process all over again.

If a couple chooses to become sexually active prior to serious consideration of values and roles, they run the risk of ending up in a genital marriage, one built on the exciting frenzy of sexual intercourse. At first it's a very enjoyable experience; both partners prioritize copulation over work, food, and sleep. They often hold the illusion that their sexual satiation is unusually special. Fed by this illusion and genital obsession, they end up married without knowing much at all about each other. It can work, but I've counseled numerous genital marriages on the rocks.

Stage five is where serious negotiations begin. You become interested in the values, lifestyle, and roles of your partner. In examining values and lifestyle, you begin to pay close attention to his or her family members, and they begin to pay close attention to you. What do you believe? Are you a Democrat or a Republican? Rich or poor? Do you brush your teeth every day? How do you dress—sloppy or neat? Do you smell good or awful? How do you handle finances and money? What is your education? Do we have anything in common? Do you smoke or abuse any substances?

If a couple finds that their values are incompatible and they continue to carry on the relationship due to genital obsession, emotional dependency, or both, they end up in a dysfunctional marriage. They may face a hard life of conflict, possible violence, separation, and divorce. If they wisely choose to end the relationship, they can return to any previous stage of mate selection and start over.

Look for a mate who will calm the turbulence in your soul rather than challenge it to battle.

Stage six deals with assumptions and expectations. If a couple finds that their values are compatible, or at least tolerable, they move to the stage where the "rubber hits the ground." When a jet touches down for a landing, the seconds of maximum danger are when the tires first hit the ground and the friction smokes clouds of burning rubber. If the tires ever blow out, it is most likely to happen at that instant of touchdown.

A farm boy raised on his mother's and sister's country cooking two or three times a day will likely go into a marriage expecting that his wife will do the cooking. Imagine the discord when she announces after the wedding, "I hate to cook. You do the cooking!" Role defining is the stage of breakthrough or breakdown in the marriage. Assumptions and expectations almost always lead to disappointments.

Two things are important to know about assumptions and expectations. First, they're usually learned in relationship to your parents. If you expect your wife to get you up in time for work, that's probably what your mother did for you. You never learned the responsibility to get up yourself. A woman who expects her husband to provide for all of her needs probably had a parent who pampered her and never allowed her to take responsibility for her own life.

The second problem with assumptions and expectations (besides the fact that they don't work) is you don't have a legitimate complaint when something you assumed or expected doesn't get done. A legitimate complaint in a relationship exists when a promise or commitment has been made. If your spouse says he will cook breakfast on Sunday mornings and then doesn't, you have a complaint. If you assume that he will cook breakfast on Sunday mornings (because that's what Dad used to do) and he doesn't, you don't have a legitimate complaint.

Mate selection is the most critical ingredient in a good marriage. Once you're in the marriage, you've bought the whole store. When couples get married, they are marrying a lot of other people—his mother and father and their mothers and fathers and their mother's and father's mothers and fathers and on it goes.

> **Marriage "is really just two scapegoats sent out by two families to reproduce each other....The battle is which one will it be."**
> **— Carl Whitaker**

Keep the Dance Alive

Date your mate and keep the dance alive! Couples need to prioritize time alone that is free of interruption. No phone calls, TV, company, children—nothing but the two of you. Be completely there for each other. Remember how much effort you put into courting each other? When you were first dating, you wouldn't have taken your mate for granted. Your hygiene was meticulous, you dressed to impress, and you strutted your stuff to win the ecstasy of private moments.

Don't stop all of this just because you're married. Marriage isn't a license to be sloppy and lazy. It's hard to create passion and attraction when you're sitting on the commode while your mate's taking a bath! Remember what you did in courtship to win her or his attention and sensual intention—and do it. Think of what you wouldn't have done, and don't do it.

The couple that plays together stays together. Play with your mate. Take time out from your busy schedules and spend time in recreation—a walk in the woods, playfully tumbling in the grass, hiking, and so on. Play is a large part of the mating dance in the animal kingdom and includes running, nudging, teasing.

Show respect and be polite. It is disrespectful to hit another human being—man, woman, child, elder. And it always involves a payback of some sort. Hitting isn't the only way to show disrespect. Words can be weapons, too.

Couples in early stages of marital therapy are surprised when I interrupt their predictable assaults and tell them that they're being disrespectful toward each other. Somewhere, somehow, they learned that it is okay to be disrespectful. Calling names, cursing, threatening, belittling, blaming, and ridiculing are all weapons of disrespect that will put a relationship in its grave. My interruption is a strategic move to shift the couple's interaction from disrespect to respect. Their disrespect is so ingrained that they aren't even aware of it. A couple wanting to work on their marriage usually will respond to this intervention.

Respect is like the backbone of mammals. Without it, we can't stand up. It contains all of the connections that coordinate the healthy functioning of our bodies. Respect in the marriage is a foundational structure that contains all of the connections within the system. To respect your mate is to honor her, to stand for her well-being and happiness.

Respect is a declaration of equality.

Both mates should encourage and support the personal and professional growth and independence of each other. A commitment is not enduring between unequals. Alfred Adler taught that to treat another person in a "less than" way does not work. "Less than" relationships lack cooperation, encouragement, and—most of all—respect.

Listen with intention. Attention in listening isn't enough. Anyone can pay attention. We pay attention to commercials, soap operas, newspapers, speeches at graduation ceremonies—but not really. If you hear a lecture or sermon and intend to discuss it with others later, you're far more likely to listen closely and grasp more than if you expect to walk away after the delivery without reviewing it.

Intentional listening is different from attentional listening. Intentional listening is the practice of at least three important skills in communication. First, you intend to understand what the other person is saying about himself or herself. You want to know what it is that the other person is saying about thinking and feeling. It's important, or that person wouldn't be talking. Even chitchat holds important messages about who people are and what they want to say to you.

Second, intend to understand the connection between what your partner says and what you say. We all carry on internal conversations. If we're to be in the conversation with the other person, we have to find something about that conversation that hooks up with our own conversations.

A final requirement for intentional listening is to listen with the intention of responding to what is being said. By giving a response, you're encouraging the other party of the conversation. Your response may be more information to consider about the topic. It sends the message that you have been listening to and thinking about what's been said.

If your response has nothing to do with the conversation, the recipient may feel devalued. Try again to get connected. Maybe you were listening and you simply didn't understand. Maybe you weren't listening, and that needs to be addressed. You are in the conversation when your internal thoughts are processing the conversation.

If you really want your partner to know what you're talking about, you have to discuss your topic in a way that connects with her or his internal conversations. Others become attentive to your conversation quickly if it has something to do with their interest.

In marriage, intend your attention to what your spouse is saying. What is she or he communicating about herself or himself? How does your spouse's conversation connect with your conversations about what he or she is saying? Talk to your spouse about what he or she is talking about. These connections can be helpful.

They also can reflect dysfunction. For example, if your wife is talking about needing some money for groceries and that triggers your thoughts about your childhood's painful poverty, you may overreact, curse, and stomp out of the house while she stands there wondering if you've lost your mind.

Fifty to a hundred bits of conversation are exchanged each second between individuals communicating actively. There is no such thing as "not communicating." Body language is a large majority of expression in communicating. If you tell your spouse you're listening while reading the newspaper, what will he or she believe about your listening—your words or your reading the newspaper? The body does not lie.

Communication takes time and practice. Don't try to talk with each other about buying a new home as you're hurrying out the door in the morning. Schedule talks. The family meeting can be one of your scheduled talk times, but also schedule time for just you and your spouse. Talking keeps the lines open for intimacy. When you encourage your mate to talk, you're encouraging the marriage to work. Without the intimacy of talking and sharing, marriages break down.

A young police officer who attended one of my seminars on stress management said that his marriage was over and he was suicidal. He said that he and his wife were barely speaking and were sleeping apart. I encouraged him to talk, and I listened with intention. For seven years, he had been chronically depressed and suicidal. He was thinking about giving up his career. His marriage was headed for divorce.

Seven years earlier, the police officer's little boy had died in his arms. The father had been holding him, trying to get him to breathe, to stay alive until they could get him to the emergency room. But the boy didn't make it. This man and his wife had never talked to anyone about their son's death, not even to each other. The grief was too unbearable, the loss devastating. Both he and his wife had vowed that they would never have another child.

"Have you ever grieved for your son?" I asked.

"No," he replied. His eyes dropped and the floodgate of seven years of not talking opened up. I encouraged him to go home and talk to his wife about his grief, the emptiness that he had felt all these years. He promised me that he would. They even visited their little boy's grave, together, for the first time since his death.

Their marriage, no longer stifled by dark silence, took on new vitality. In a phone call two years later, he excitedly said, "I wanted you to know that my wife and I are seven months pregnant. I'm going back to law school, and we're happy! Thanks for listening and the encouragement. It still hurts, but life isn't over yet!"

Break Old Habits of Interaction

Break the old habits of interaction that you learned from your parents and other adults in your life. You're already working on this by reading this book. The information you are receiving provides the opportunity for a new way of thinking about old habits and patterns of behavior that don't work.

You can change your being! It will be hard work, but it also will be rewarding, forward progress. You'll be happier and healthier when you choose not to be angry for days, weeks, even months and choose to resolve conflict in a nonviolent way. How to change will be dealt with more specifically later in this chapter. It isn't so much that you're going to be a new person; you will be you forever. But you can change your behaviors, attitudes, and choices.

One immediate change is to practice being less serious about your mate's and your own emotions. If he gets depressed, that doesn't mean you have to get depressed. If he gets angry, that doesn't mean you have to get angry. Practice not getting involved in the other person's conflict. If she's in the middle of an emotional outburst, get out of the way. Take the sails out of the winds of conflict. You don't have to get involved in every conflict or problem that comes up.

Don't take life or your relationship so seriously. Be careful about criticizing your spouse's faults. Remember that they may have prevented her or him from getting a better mate.

Be a Friend and Companion

An original use of the term *companionate love* described a relationship free of eternal entrapment. It meant that either or both parties could end their marriage by mutual consent if they were childless and basically bored.[7]

This narrow view of companionate love is off the mark. Companionate love is captured in Kahlil Gibran's teachings on marriage in *The Prophet*:

> **Then Almitra spoke again and said, "And what of marriage, master?"**
>
> **And he answered saying: "You were born together, and together you shall be forevermore. You shall be together when the white winds of death scatter your days.**
>
> **Ay, you shall be together even in the silent memory of God. But let there be spaces in your togetherness,**
>
> **And let the winds of the heavens dance between you. Love one another, but make not a bond of love:**
>
> **Let it rather be a moving sea between the shores of your souls. Fill each other's cup but drink not from one cup.**

**Give one another of your bread but eat not from
the same loaf. Sing and dance together and be
joyous, but let each one of you be alone.**

**Even as the strings of a lute are alone though they
quiver with the same music. Give your hearts, but
not into each other's keeping.**

**For only the hand of life can contain your hearts.
And stand together yet not too near together:**

For the pillars of the temple stand apart,

**And the oak tree and the cypress grow not in each
other's shadow.**[8]

Companionate love is the discovery of your mate as a good friend and companion, a movement that takes a long time. As James Kavanaugh writes in *A Fable*, "It is a gentle force like the river making smooth the rough edges of rocks. Love cannot invade like an avalanche in the mountains or the north wind which topples the cypress."[9]

Eros is great, a flaming start for marriage. It isn't lost in companionate love; it's simply put in its proper perspective. It is seen as a beautiful engagement of your souls in a joyful, chosen union. We are to celebrate the brilliance of sex. It is so enjoyable that it ensures the continuation of the species. But after the initial flame goes out, what's next? Divorce and a re-creation of the initial flame with someone else? That's a possibility; even so, such a cycle would also flame out. Sooner or later, you have to settle down and either stay with your chosen mate or live alone.

What's next is a move into a relationship of respect, friendship, and love. True love will open our hearts. Having a companion who is a good friend is the greatest reward of marriage. Conversations are not laced with reactive concerns of low self-esteem and paranoia. Instead, two adults support and are interested in each other. There is no violence, no screaming hatred and anger. Instead there is mutual respect, an honoring of self and the other. This is a tremendously healthy setting in which to raise children.

**It takes guts to stay married. There will be many
crises between the wedding day and the golden anni-
versary, and the people who make it are heroes.**
—Howard Whitman

MAKING PARENTING WORK

To lose hope for a child is the same as to stop watering plants although one wishes them to grow.
—Alfred Adler

BETTER PARENTS CALLED KEY
TO SOLVING TEENS' PROBLEMS

Chicago—After 400 community meetings to examine what ails the nation's youths, a national commission has found broad agreement on the No. 1 solution to the problem: better parents.

The urgent need for parents to do a better job in raising their children was a "universal theme" in communities from Carlsbad, California, to Lewiston, Maine, to Snellville, Georgia.

Every high school should start teaching teens to be good parents.

A telephone operator gets more training than a parent.
—Betsy White, *Atlanta Journal/Constitution*, April 6, 1990

I continue to be amazed by parents who consistently bring their children to therapy to be fixed, wondering why their children are angry and out of control—and they have hit, spanked, screamed at, belittled, and threatened their kids, locked them in solitary confinement for hours, and generally abused the kids.

Angry? Children who are hit and emotionally abused become enraged. Overwhelmed by the giant parent who can physically do just about anything he or she wants to do, the child tucks away his or her rage until the opportunity comes to express it. A basic rule about hitting your child is that the child will always find a way to balance the scale.

With few exceptions, parents love their kids. This includes abusive parents. Except in cases of mentally ill parents, abuse is not usually the result of hate or malice aforethought. It is the result of unskilled parents repeating what they learned. The most common statement made by parents who bring me their angry children is, "No, I don't hit my child! Of course, I spank him, but there's nothing wrong with that!"

Parent education is a painstakingly slow process. Many par-

112

ents simply don't want to take responsibility for their child's behavior. So the kids are carted off to psychologists and psychiatrists to be diagnosed and treated for attention deficit disorders, enuresis, antisocial behavior, and worse. What parents actually are saying is, "Give us a patient in the family. Don't tell us that we are responsible for the problem!"

Family therapy is pioneering new ways of thinking about parent-child relationships. The application of the parenting skills in this section will work if practiced consistently and with a commitment to never hit your child again. That includes spanking. A primary goal in improving parent-child relations is to make the home safe for the children in it.

Let's review why hitting doesn't work. First of all, *spanking establishes a "less than" relationship* in which children are taught that adults are bigger and, therefore, right. Yet many behaviors of the child that are punished are behaviors of the parent as well. In other words, the child gets punished for what he or she learned from the parent. This doesn't make sense to the child.

Second, *hitting a child makes the child angry* and always results in some sort of payback. It perpetuates a vicious cycle. The child retaliates with more misbehavior. The parent spanks the child again for that misbehavior, and so on. A cruel parent will push this cycle until the child's spirit is broken, and—just like a whipped dog—the child will go through life with severe fear and low self-esteem. When the abused children grow up, they repeat the cycle on their own children.

When parents make a commitment to stop hitting their children, they are making a commitment to give their future grandchildren a safe environment.

Why is it all right to hit children when it isn't all right to hit adults?

A mother in Alabama tried to press charges against a vice principal for paddling her seven-year-old for shouting on the bus. Lawyers said she had no case. In a moment of anger, the mother struck the vice principal with the paddle he had used. She was charged with assault with a "deadly weapon" and faced up to ten years in jail if convicted, as reported in *Working Mother* in January 1988. The mother was convicted and received a sentence of six months in jail and four-and-a-half years' probation!

Spanking a child with his or her pants down is a violation of healthy sexual development and well-being. It borders on incestuous behavior and violates the child's dignity. Parents and teachers need to put themselves in the place of the child. How would adults feel if a spouse, a personnel manager, or the school principal pulled their pants down, bent them over their knees or chair, and spanked them? It certainly could be seen as having sexual content; so what's the difference with children?

Another thing that hitting does is to set a poor example of handling conflict and problems. Children learn by observing adults in their world. If it's okay for parents and teachers to hit them, it must be all right for them to hit people, too.

The National Parent-Teachers Association (PTA) published a bulletin saying that corporal punishment teaches:

- might makes right;
- it's okay to strike out in anger;
- we control others by force;
- the way to let out dissatisfaction is by physically abusing others;
- low self-esteem, a feeling that "it's okay for others to hit me";
- hurt and humiliation that is often out of proportion to the misbehavior; and
- fear and resentment of authority.[10]

This last result of hitting bears repeating. Hitting your children establishes an "authority figure problem" that will plague them for most of their lives. How can children trust authority figures when the most important authority figures in their lives—parents and teachers—hit them?

Dr. Cameron Meredith, an Adlerian mentor in family therapy, gives a challenge to parents with the question: "Do you have the courage to let your child have the freedom to be, rather than controlling them to be?"

The following information on parenting skills will take courage to practice. Old habits are hard to break, for they've been rehearsed for most of your life. New skills have to be practiced over and over again. You can expect some slips along the way. Stay committed to a new and more effective way of parenting and you'll reap the results you seek.

Parenting Skills

Education

Educating yourself as a parent is the beginning of a new life. Parenting 101 as a high school course does not exist. When we buy a new car, it comes with a descriptive operation and maintenance manual. With just about every major merchandise transaction in our culture, we receive a book of instructions. But when we have a baby? Maybe a cigar, a blue or pink ribbon on our mailbox, Pampers galore, and baby clothes—but certainly no instruction manual. The most important entree of life comes with no book of instructions.

Parents today need education in child development and management. Read as many books on the topic as possible. Pay attention to the author's point of view on important issues. For example, if you're wanting information about sex education, seek reliable sources. Take parenting classes, such as Active Parenting. Join parent support groups. Do everything you can to learn as much as you can about your children and parenting.

Purposeful Behavior

Misbehavior stems from four basic causes: attention, power, revenge, and inadequacy. Teenagers and adults add two other causes for misbehavior: excitement and perfection.

Attention-getting misbehavior. Some people believe that they count only when others notice them, are kept busy with them, and give them service. These kids are center stage in the family and society. They will do anything to keep the attention focused on them. The child is angry and makes a statement about it in the way he dresses, talks, walks, and behaves. The peace sign of the sixties often was replaced with the "bird" sign of frustration and protestation. If you're not paying attention, or if you're doing something that the child does not like, he or she will get your attention one way or another.

One way to deal with attention-getting misbehavior is to ignore it while it is happening. Wait until later, when the child is doing something useful and is behaving appropriately. Move in and thank him or her for the good behavior. Let the child know how much you appreciate it. You want to reinforce positive behaviors and give little or no attention to the negative behaviors.

For example, when a child is throwing a temper tantrum, if you move in and try to stop it, you usually end up throwing a temper tantrum yourself. You yell, threaten, even hit to stop the tantrum. This only adds to the misbehavior and gives the attention being sought—so it will be repeated again. You can count on it. Children learn quickly what works and what doesn't work with their parents. If you simply leave the room or walk away from the fury of the child, he or she will stop sooner or later. No child has been known to scream forever.

Concerned parents ask, "But what if my child hurts himself? He gets so violent, even bangs his head against the wall." What is the purpose of the child's behavior? If it's attention, then don't feed it. He or she will stop when no one is attending to the tantrum. Depending on the child's age level, it is unlikely that he or she will continue banging for long after losing the attention sought. If the child is very young, distraction—without giving in to what the child wants—works best. For example, if your young child is throwing a tantrum over a cookie, turn on TV cartoons or bring the puppy inside for a few minutes.

A child who seeks attention through misbehavior is making the statement, "Nobody knows I'm around. I'd better make certain they know I count for something around here!" Make your child feel noticed and important. Do things as simple as a bedtime ritual where you say to the child: "Good night. I love you. You're my favorite six-year-old girl in the whole wide world."

Power struggles. Parents who step into power struggles set up by their kids cannot win. Children cannot be made to do anything. Anytime you set up a conversation where they can say no and you want them to say yes, you can lose. Even if they're punished and coerced into saying what you want to hear, they can still say no internally—and win.

Power struggles are children's way of getting others to do what they want them to do. They operate on an attitude of, "No I won't do it and you can't make me." This misbehavior can show up in aggressive behavior that bullies playmates and siblings. Don't play into their game. They know the turf and they will use it well. Parents who take on or give in to power struggles with their kids eventually will lose!

The best way to deal with power-seeking misbehavior is to declare victory and withdraw. In a power struggle, we want to create a double-win situation with no losers. This can be done by asking for the child's help or contribution. If you feel angry about the child's behavior, remove yourself from the situation in a friendly way. Do not move back into the situation until you decide not to be angry.

You may have been taught by your parents to move in to the thick of the battle and take no prisoners. To do so may win a temporary victory, but it won't last. Anytime there is a loser, there is the desire to win the next time and never to let the victor win again. With power struggles, we should neither fight children nor give in to their demands.

Revenge. Children who use revenge as a motive for misbehavior feel hurt by life and believe that the solution is to hurt others as they've been hurt. They are future codependents! In working with Vietnam veterans, my clinical experience reveals that many of those who are suffering from post-traumatic stress disorder live in a childlike state of punishing revenge.

Children caught up in vengeful behavior believe that life is unfair and feel sorry for themselves. Abused children frequently use this type of misbehavior to pay back the injustice of being hit or molested. When I get the parent(s) to agree to stop hitting the child and to tell the child about this commitment, the child will go through a brief period of hitting or punishing the parent(s). It's a payback they've always wanted to do but never felt safe enough. I advise parents to keep their commitment and talk with the child about how it feels to be hit, and to apologize for all the times that they had hit the child. I ask them to inform their child that, together, they will be learning some new skills in being a family and learning what choices they have instead of hitting.

How do you deal with revengeful misbehavior? To strike back or react to the vengeful child is to return revenge for revenge. It only reinforces the child's view of life as unfair: "See, I knew you were mean and spiteful! I knew you would hit me even though you said you were going to stop!"

Do not strike back out of anger and hurt feelings. As in the power struggle, it is best to withdraw until later and find a time of good behavior to move back in to encourage and support the child.

Inadequacy and withdrawal. Inadequacy is a misbehavior of discouragement. The child is so discouraged that he or she does not want to do anything. She or he wants to be left alone. This child wants to avoid all demands or expectations, especially by adults. Such children usually are victimized by parents who expect too much and are constantly nagging and haranguing them to do whatever they're doing, only better. Parents of inadequate children have difficulty leaving the child alone and send consistent criticizing and discouraging messages.

In turn, discouraged children become experts at convincing adults of their inadequacies, even to the point of playing along with concerns about their intelligence or attention span. They play out the role of the family's identified patient. I've seen, for example, a child diagnosed as having attention-deficit disorder (ADD), squirm and not sit still for a fifty-minute family therapy session, but at the same time report that he watched cartoons on TV last Saturday morning for five straight hours!

Dr. Tim Evans, an Adlerian family therapist at the University of Georgia, says, "Trying to motivate a person whose goal is inadequacy is like pushing a tractor out of a swamp. The more you push, the more he sinks."[11]

How do you deal with inadequacy and withdrawal as the goal of misbehavior? Those children who use inadequacy lack courage. Rudolph Dreikurs says, "This courage can only come from encouragement and a willingness to believe in them no matter how hard they try to prove us wrong."[12]

With this inadequacy behavior, we should never give up on the child. We must persist in communicating our belief and trust in the child's ability to function and contribute, to be responsible. Believing in the child who no longer believes in his or her own self-worth is highly encouraging to the child.

A lot of time and energy could be saved by parents if they simply would learn to leave their kids alone. Stop trying to control their lives. They are separate human beings who have the right to design their own lives. Certainly, you can coach and assist with guidelines, rules, and encouragement. But let them help set the goals.

My advocating this distancing often is met with stunned resistance. "What do you mean? She can't get up by herself in the morning. I have to call her a dozen times just to get her feet to touch the floor. She'd be late for school. She'd miss breakfast."

So what? She will learn to get out of bed all by herself if you'll just leave her alone. Five- to seven-year-old kids can learn to get themselves out of bed in the morning in time for breakfast and kindergarten—but it's not going to happen if we continue to do everything for them. It's no wonder many of our kids today feel inadequate!

Excitement as a goal of misbehavior. Everyone loves excitement. But when the goal of misbehavior is excitement, children or teenagers escalate their risks and can get into serious trouble. They are in danger of harming themselves or others. Speeding, driving on the wrong side of the road, running stop signs, sniffing glue, promiscuity, and daredevil games are a few of the high-cost risks involved.

How do you deal with excitement as a goal of misbehavior? Don't play the game by repeatedly pointing out the consequences of misbehavior for excitement. Once is enough. Teenagers must see the cost of the behavior for themselves. You cannot change it for them; your task is to establish boundaries and stay out of the way of the misbehaviors, to accept the individual while not accepting the behaviors that are self- and other-destructive. Encourage safe, acceptable alternatives when the thrill seeker is ready to listen.

Your background of relationship with your child is so important at this time. Parents who have been out of synchronization with their children for years cannot expect suddenly to have control and influence on a teenager. Parents who find themselves at this stage, with little influence, need to seek professional help at once. Excitement seekers take great risks to feel the "rush" they become addicted to experiencing.

Perfectionism. Children can develop this mistaken goal, thinking that they will be accepted and okay when they are perfect. They equate winning with being accepted. Since the reality is that no one wins all the time, these kids feel like failures. They tend to be underachievers. In order to be perfect, they take on tasks below their capability. This is done to avoid failure and unacceptable mistakes. The perfectionist child attempts as little as possible in order to maintain the ability to do things correctly.

Perfectionist kids also are judgmental and critical of their parents and peers. No one can do anything right. The more they can prove your inadequacies, the better they feel about themselves. They are not very much fun to be around.

How do you deal with perfectionist misbehavior? This is a tough one! Herein is the embodiment of addictive behaviors, such as anorexia nervosa and bulimia (eating disorders), alcohol and other drug addiction, and obsessive-compulsive behaviors. Don't criticize these children and embrace them when they fail. Stop expecting them to do everything right. Don't overreact when they succeed, and let them know that it is only human to make mistakes. Remember, there are no bad children, no bad teenagers, only discouraged kids!

Encouragement

Encouragement is an act of giving courage. Children of courage cooperate with their siblings and parents and are responsible for their choices and actions. Courageous children have encouraging parents!

The principle behind encouragement is believing in your children, whether they make straight A's or C's. Encouragement is a way of saying to your child, "You are enough! You're absolutely wonderful the way you are." Discouragement throws in a few "ifs": "If you make all A's, you'll get fifty dollars." "If you get a base hit, I'll give you a bonus on your allowance." "If you behave, we'll get some ice cream." Encouragement instills cooperation without expectations of rewards. It also avoids the loss of self-esteem when the child doesn't get all A's or a base hit and behaves poorly.

On the average, children receive thirty to fifty discouraging statements a day from parents and teachers. I remember vividly the day that my seven-year-old daughter came home from school in tears. In an art project, she had used two pieces of paper instead of one piece of paper as instructed. Her enthusiasm was rewarded by having her name written on the board as punishment!

Encourage your children at every opportunity. Acknowledge the positive, overlook the negative, and focus on providing the democratic environment in which they can learn to be responsible, self-sufficient human beings. Begin early in their lives to encourage them to make decisions. Let them choose which cereals to eat, clothes to wear, toys to take on a trip, and purchases to make with their allowances.

Don't nag them! Tell your children what needs to be done only once. Alfred Adler's son, Kurt Adler, says that parents' "nagging repetition teaches a child only not to listen!" He says that you should avoid telling a child what to do. Instead, you should say to the child, "Here, let's do this together." You teach cooperation by example, by cooperating with the child!

Share responsibilities and don't give your children all the jobs you don't want to do. Let them decide which chores to do. Parents who give their kids all the "dirty work" wonder why their kids don't carry their fair share. Take turns at carrying out the garbage and mowing the yard. Mix it up to be fair.

Let the child do the job without intervention—unless, of course, it involves his or her safety. Stay out of it, even when you see that it could be done more quickly and efficiently. A fifteen-minute job may take your seven-year-old an hour to accomplish, but you'll have a courageous seven-year-old if you'll just leave him or her alone.

I remember my incredible sense of accomplishment when I was a young boy and my brother-in-law let me drive his John Deere tractor for the first time. At first, Gene rode on the back of it to make certain I was able to reach all of the instruments and knew what I was doing. When he stood back and said, "Go to it," I drove up and down that Missouri farm road for hours.

Don't compare your children with each other or with other children. Comparison sets up competition and feelings of inadequacy. Let them know that they are accepted as they are, that each one of them is a VIP (very important person) in the family and in their school. Be sure that they know that everyone else is a VIP, or else you'll have a perfectionist child on your hands.

The point of encouraging your child is to instill courage instead of discouragement. To do this, you will need to decide to be an encouraging person. If you were raised in a dysfunctional family, you are probably in the habit of being discouraging, critical, and judgmental. If you want to change, then you will need to monitor carefully what you say. To learn the new behavior of being positive rather than critical will take time and effort on your part. It's worth it. Not only will you be helping your children thrive, you'll also be more pleasant to others and will notice more good in life.

Encouragers are accepting of themselves and everyone around them. Their spouse and children love to be with them and live in a playful, courageous environment. Everyone feels a sense of belonging. Children feel supported and believed in. Encouraging parents are optimists. An encourager once said, "I'd rather be optimistic and wrong than pessimistic and right!" Encouraging parents affirm their children and are affectionate, compassionate, and forgiving with them.

Discouraging parents are judgmental, critical, angry, and looking for mistakes. They're physically and verbally abusive. They're bad news people, focusing on the negative side of life. "Gloom, despair, and agony—all three" is their theme song, and their children don't have a chance at developing courage!

Parents have to choose which attitude they'll adopt. One might think that family violence and discouragement can be explained in terms of cause and effect. Though understanding some roots of dysfunctional behavior is helpful, stopping family violence requires a new way of thinking. No longer can we accept that we are victims of the past in Freudian causality. We must be the choosers of who we are in the present, regardless of the past. Instead of being pushed by the past, we are pulled by the present to be responsible for our choices. Our choice to stop family violence must include encouragement.

> **You know you are an encourager when you like**
> **yourself. You know you like yourself when things**
> **go poorly and you're still gentle with yourself.**[13]
> —Dr. Tim Evans

Remember, discouragement is at the root of all misbehavior. I encourage parents in a dysfunctional family to work on monitoring their own behavior. Think of your brain as the camera that monitors every move you make in your local bank—your entry, your clothing, the way you look, tone of voice. The bank monitor doesn't miss anything. It works for a safe environment and records any actions of would-be or actual perpetrators. When beginning to change from being a discourager to an encourager, you will need a monitoring system.

Last year I took my five-year-old son on a fishing trip in a canoe down the Chattahoochee. The day started off wrong, with overcast skies threatening rain and not-so-clear water polluted with silt from a nearby gold-mining company. In the first small rapids, we almost tipped over. My fishing line got scrambled in the bushes while going through the second rapids. Kyffon's reel backlashed into chaotic tangles, and he had to relieve himself.

In those first thirty minutes, I heard my voice raising and being critical of everything, including my son. My monitor flashed a red flag with the conversation that said, You're being just like your parents were when they were discouraged and angry over the Depression and hard times. Here I sit being discouraged and angry over things not going the way I want them to!

I looked at the sadness and discouragement on my son's face and then changed what was happening. I apologized to Kyffon, told him that nothing that had happened was his fault and that we were going to have a great day on the river. His face lit up. By day's end, he had caught several fish (without Daddy's interfering) and we had enjoyed a day of encouragement, affection, and mutual respect.

Our internal monitor is like a computer. It carries on conversations about what we're saying and doing. If we learn to pay attention to its messages, we can change the way we choose to be. We can stop discouraging conversations. The monitor helps us be responsible for our word choices. Martin Heidegger referred to language as the "house of our being."

Children learn how to live from how adults live. Dorothy Law Nolte has captured the essence of what I am saying about encouragement:

> **If a child lives with criticism**
> **he learns to condemn.**
>
> **If a child lives with hostility**
> **he learns to fight.**
>
> **If a child lives with ridicule**
> **he learns to be shy.**
>
> **If a child lives with shame**
> **he learns to feel guilty.**
>
> **If a child lives with tolerance**
> **he learns to be patient.**
>
> **If a child lives with encouragement**
> **he learns confidence.**
>
> **If a child lives with praise**
> **he learns to appreciate.**
>
> **If a child lives with fairness**
> **he learns justice.**
>
> **If a child lives with security**
> **he learns to have faith.**
>
> **If a child lives with approval**
> **he learns to like himself.**
>
> **If a child lives with acceptance and friendship**
> **he learns to find love in the world.**

Time

American parents give their children an average of ten minutes or less focused individual attention each day. School and TV give the most attention! This must change.

Children need individual attention from each parent. I recommend one hour a day, every day, with each child. Busy parents will protest; but if you don't spend time with your kids, someone else will. You'll miss out on the most important, enjoyable stages of your children's lives. Help design your children's lives in intentional ways. By your absence, inattention, and selective criticisms, you'll miss being a positive contributor to your children. They'll be all right without your involvement, but they'll be better with it.

Our society is beginning to see the effects of latchkey children and unsupervised, unencouraged kids who grow up with a sense of not belonging. For kids to feel encouraged by their parents, they need their presence and time. This side of encouragement—time—is one of the most important things you can give your kids. It lets them know they're worthwhile.

Discipline without Spanking

"So what do I do if I can't spank my child?" "Not spank? He'll never do what I want him to now." Parents who learned spanking as a normal way of discipline have difficulty changing. Their internal monologues about spanking justify its use. To break the habit, new perspectives and parenting skills are needed to replace the old. Being disciplined should help the child develop healthy attitudes. *Discipline should be for the good of the child, not the parent's convenience.* The goal of discipline is to teach responsibility to rules and boundaries between acceptable and unacceptable behavior.

> **But the Bible says, He who spares the rod hates his son, but he who loves him is careful to discipline him.**
> **—Proverbs 13:24**

Several years ago, a news article headline stated, "He beats up kids for the glory of God." The article described the death of a child in a religious commune. In another case, when one father was confronted by the state child protection workers, he resisted their assistance and said,

"What do you mean I can't beat my child? I'm a Christian!"

One day, I took my children shopping with me to a furniture warehouse where a young man was working on the front door awning. My son was disgruntled about something and let me know of his displeasure.

The young man on the ladder frowned and said, "Use the Bible on him and he'll straighten out."

"What do you mean?" I asked.

He said, "Spare the rod, spoil the child! He just needs a good beatin' and he'll straighten up real quick!"

He was stunned when I told him that I didn't believe in hitting children. He said, "Not even spanking?"

"Not even spanking."

"Mister," he said, "you need to read the Bible!"

I've read the Bible at least a dozen times through (from cover to cover, since I'm a recovering compulsive myself). This passage quoted is one that needs clarification! It has done more harm than good. Advocates of corporal punishment often misquote this particular text. They don't quote scriptural reports of child sacrifices and incest or any other controversial information in the Old Testament. They choose the scriptures that fit their point of view.

In the first place, the shepherd's rod was used for two main purposes: for guiding sheep and for counting sheep at day's end. The shepherd's rod was not used for beating sheep! If a young lamb strayed from the flock, the shepherd would reach out with the rod and guide the lamb back within safe boundaries. At night, he would use the rod for counting by gently tapping each sheep as it entered the chosen resting place.

To spare the rod would be the equivalent of a permissive style of parenting, one that provides no significant guidance and direction. Children from permissive homes grow up irresponsible and spoiled.

In the Bible, a shepherd is a very positive character. He would carry wounded lambs in his arms and lead gently those ewes that were with young (Isaiah 40:11). The shepherd's gentleness was shown in his ministering to the sick and guiding the straying animal back to safety. He was constantly with his flock. He would patiently seek out the lost, the disabled, the frightened sheep. If he was slack in watchfulness, they were likely to become scattered. If he was not so keen in his attention, they were more apt to be lost. If he was easily excited, they were more apt to be hard to guide. The flock reflected the shepherd.

Children reflect their parents. A minister's daughter once returned home at three o'clock in the morning from a dance. Her father greeted her sternly, "Good morning, child of the devil!"

With humor, she replied, "Good morning, Father."

The Twenty-third Psalm reflects the caring uses of the shepherd's rod by, "Thy rod and thy staff, they comfort me."

Goals of parenting are to provide safe boundaries and accountability. To spare the rod means to not provide guidance. *It has nothing to do with hitting.* We have to be very careful about well-meaning people who use their faith as a justification for what they've learned through their own family experience. The young man working on the awning likely was beaten as a child. Unless he learns new attitudes, he is likely to beat his own children, too, espousing scripture between licks. It's a tragic use of the Bible and a tragic abuse of children!

To have options available in stressful times helps relieve the pressure and moderates your reactions to your misbehaving child. The options that follow are designed to provide a safe home for you and your children, free of hitting and angry outbursts.

Time-out. One important alternative to spanking is *time-out*. Time-out is an effective use of allowing the child time to reflect about unacceptable behavior. It also interrupts the behavior and ensuing crisis. It should be done in a hallway or room devoid of toys and TV, but within contact of the family. Time-out does *not* mean solitary confinement in a locked closet or room. One minute per year of age is a good rule—six minutes for six-year-olds, and so on. Explain to the child why he or she is in time-out.

A second advantage of using time-out is that it gives you, the parent, time-out, too. You're giving yourself time to calm down, reflect, and come back to the problem more rationally.

Distraction is more effective with younger children. Time-out is not recommended for toddlers and preschoolers. Distraction is a technique of using your child's natural curiosity to shift the focus from misbehavior. If you focus on the unwanted behavior, you are likely to get locked in a power struggle with a little warrior. The world of the child is exciting, and every moment brings discovery of something new. If the discovery is dangerous or not acceptable, interrupt it with something else that's safe and acceptable.

Prevention is a helpful skill in distraction. Try to anticipate trouble and distract the child before it arrives. Don't let your child do something that is dangerous or self-destructive in order to learn a lesson. Parental intervention is necessary, for example, in teaching kids about the street and crosswalk safety. Cross streets with them and have them decide when to cross. Intervene when they make a dangerous choice and explain why.

Instead of spanking, establish logical consequences of misbehavior. Let the child participate in deciding what the logical consequences will be. Logical consequences are not punitive in nature, but are the results of our actions. They can be positive or negative, depending on the behavior. An adolescent who comes home after an established curfew can expect to have his or her curfew hour made earlier the following weekend. A teenage driver who gets a speeding ticket can be forewarned that car privileges will change as a result of the ticket. Consistency is important in order for logical consequences to work. Responsibility within boundaries is a goal of logical consequences.

Natural consequences do not have to be established. They already exist. If you touch fire, you get burned. They are always effective. A child who touches a hot stove will not do it again. Parental intervention may be necessary for the child's safety. You don't want your child to touch a hot stove so he or she can learn about fire.

Who owns the problem? This question is one of the most helpful questions that parents can discover. Parents get sucked into their kids' problems before realizing that they don't need to get involved. Not every problem your child faces is yours. When Susan comes crying to you saying that it's her turn to choose the game, give ownership of the problem back to the children involved.

Teach problem-solving techniques, which can enhance your children's ability to cope. And then let them practice those techniques. Identify who owns the problem before setting yourself up as judge and jury. You don't have to solve every problem! Tell Susan to go work it out with her brother, that you trust her ability to handle the situation. Intervene only if the situation gets out of hand. Do you want your children growing up depending on others to solve their problems, or being self-reliant in handling most problems that come their way?

If the problem is the child's problem, encourage him or her to think of solutions to correct the situation: "I'm sorry you don't like picking up your toys in the living room. What can you do to make it more fun?" If the problem is between you and the child, take the opportunity to be fair and work it out so that you both have some of your needs met. The older the child, the more you can invite participation in considering solutions.

Compromise is a necessary survival skill.

Allow your children to help you. Let them know that they can be a big help to Daddy or Mommy. Let them drive nails their own way without constant instruction. This winter, while I was splitting wood with a sledge hammer and wedges, my six-year-old son wanted to try it. At first, I had these conversations go on inside my head:

"No, it's impossible, Son; you're too little."

"No, the sledge hammer's too heavy for you."

"No, you'll miss the wedges and hurt yourself."

"No, you'll strain yourself."

"No, it'll take too long, and I'm in a hurry."

Fortunately, I canned all of those conversations except the one about safety and said, "Sure, Son, go ahead." With a few simple instructions on safety and getting the wedges started for him, I stood back. He struggled to lift the sledge hammer a foot or so above the shank, but it came down with a satisfying metal-to-metal click! I watched in amazement while my son split several pieces of wood. When he was exhausted, he handed the sledge hammer back to me, with considerable satisfaction and a smile on his face.

Don't do for a child what he or she can do alone.

When you make mistakes, be open and honest with your children. Tell them that you made a mistake and that you're sorry. When we apologize and ask forgiveness, we are telling our children that we are human, too. We also are setting an excellent example of behavior we want to see in them. Admitting your errors allows forgiveness and closeness to develop.

Play more and be affectionate. One of my fonder memories is sitting in my father's lap and rocking alongside the static-filled radio listening to "Ozzie and Harriet." His unshaven face was rough and he smelled like sweaty cattle and hay. I remember his laughter that pleasantly interrupted his stress-filled day of hard labor as a renter on that corn, beef, and produce farm in northwest Missouri. What I remember most is being held.

Children need your affection. Hug them, kiss them, look directly into their eyes and tell them how much you love them and appreciate the gift of having them as your children. Spend time playing games with them, reading to them; enter into their world for a while. Think of it as creating memories you want them to have that will help make their lives and their children's lives more meaningful and enjoyable.

Family Meetings

A family is where children learn about our society. We live in a democratic society. If our families are autocratic, our children may revolt. To avoid the fireworks of a domestic declaration of independence day, we need to be as democratic as our society. A democratic home will provide the optimum training environment for launching our children into the world.

A family council meeting is a parenting tactic that works. (If spouse abuse is a problem, use caution in trying this concept. Abusers could find this forum threatening and lash out at their victims.) A family meeting involves shared leadership and the development of decision-making skills for all family members. Held on a regular basis, the family meeting provides an ongoing opportunity for every member to have a say about family rules and dilemmas.

A family council meeting is established with the following suggestions:

- Meet regularly and keep minutes.

- Don't meet for more than one hour, as the mind will retain only what the butt can endure. Children's attention spans rarely tolerate more than thirty minutes of anything except play.

- Stick to the agenda. Keep an agenda sheet posted throughout the week on the refrigerator. Any family member can write on it a concern or problem to be dealt with at the next meeting.

- Share leadership. Whoever takes minutes will be the chairperson of the next meeting. Children old enough to write and take minutes (usually age six and above) will share in the chair.

- Begin each meeting with compliments and affirmations. This gets things started on a positive note.

- Read the minutes from the last meeting and deal with financial matters—allowances, purchases, and so on. Children, however, do not need to be burdened with near bankruptcy details or house payments. Discuss finances appropriate to age levels.

- Handle old business and new business by asking everyone to participate. Brainstorm together and listen closely to everyone. After you have brainstormed a problem together, move to problem-solving suggestions and vote on a solution. Whoever is involved in the solution will need to make a commitment to it.

- Some problems will not be resolved in one or two meetings. Let them remain on the agenda under old business and keep coming back to them. This teaches your children that not all problems need to be or can be solved quickly. The democratic process takes time.

- Close the meeting with affirmations and a review of the work accomplished.[14]

The idea of a family meeting where every child has a voice is an unfamiliar idea to families of violence and addiction. Control, punishment, and threats create havoc and breakdown.

Family violence tragically affects the formative years of a child's most impressionable period of development. Let's give our children the best beginning seven years of their lives, and the world will be a better place for everyone.

A democracy allows change and freedom of speech. Be ready for both! At a recent family council meeting, I found myself becoming irritated with the agenda. My ten-year-old stepdaughter was moderating the meeting, and our eight-year-old daughter was taking minutes. Keily asked for the agenda.

Keily began, with eyes flashing toward my direction, and said, "The first item on the agenda is Daddy."

I could handle that.

"He needs to work on his yelling."

"Yelling! I don't yell."

"It's yelling to us," piped in six-year-old Kyffon.

"Yeh, Daddy, and we don't like it," said Autumn.

"Okay, I thought I had been doing pretty well with this, but I obviously need to work even harder."

Democracy works, but it can be challenging. Encouraged children are challenging because they are courageous. Don't encourage your children if you can't stand the courage!

Alfred Adler once said that courage is the greatest gift that a parent can give a child. It gives our children courage when they see that what they say matters. To have a part in family decisions and conversations about the home environment and rules prepares them for having a part in society's decisions and conversations about its environment and rules. The family meeting gives the children a positive view of themselves and others and a sense of belongingness that will serve them well throughout their lives.

Our society gets what we give in the home.

EMPOWERMENT FOR CHANGE

As for grownups, is there any likelihood that we may be able to mold ourselves into something better than we are?

—Will Durant

Stopping family violence hinges on the answer to this question. If the answer is no, family violence will continue. But if the answer is yes, family violence can be stopped. And we all can mold ourselves into something better than we are!

However, it will take a major commitment and considerable effort to practice new ways of being while stopping old habits and internal conversations. It will take a new awareness that we are the designers of our thoughts, words, and actions. We choose our attitudes about life. They do not happen to us; we happen to them.

This section requires your willingness, interest, and intention to change. Do you want to change your life? If so, you are invited to shift your attention and intention to a heightened level of being.

This heightened level of being represents an experience of metanoia, a turning-around-upside-down-inside-out new way of thinking. Rather than obsessing on analysis of the past or projections of the future, you are called into the present moment of awareness with a new intensity.

The intensity required is similar to the experience of canoeing the Chauga River in South Carolina. Being an amateur "river rat," I've whitewater canoed several rivers with class three and four rapids like "the Edge of the World" and "Bull's Sluice." They all require your complete attention and exhaust you by day's end.

The Chauga River is in a class all by itself. It isn't paddled by many canoeing enthusiasts. The river demands two lengthy and exhausting portages around waterfalls and the current is strong and swift. In order to maneuver your canoe, you have to paddle at a more intense level than ever before. What works on most rivers won't work on this one.

Stopping family violence also requires a deeper and more intense level of awareness and commitment. This section on empowerment for change has strange formations and strong currents of change. You may want to read it several times to absorb what challenges and interests you the most. Be creative with the information—experiment with it.

Try to connect the nine dots of this puzzle with four lines without duplicating any line or lifting your pen from the page.

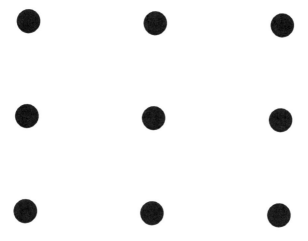

In writing this book, I take a stand for stopping family violence. This is a major task of changing our way of thinking and being. To bring about these changes, a new level of conversation is required, one that goes outside the normal context of our thinking and being. This nine-dot exercise is an example of how we limit the way we think about problem solving. Look now at the solution. It can be resolved only by going outside the limits of the dot box! As long as you stay inside, it is impossible to solve.

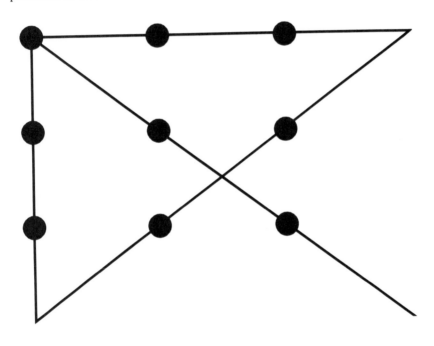

The same is true of family violence. If we stay inside the usual perimeters of problem solving, family violence cannot be stopped. It will require going outside the limits to a new level of thinking and being.

**The one freedom you have at all times and under
any circumstances is to choose your attitude.**
—Alfred Adler

Attitudes about parenting and family life are learned, but we are responsible for what we learn. We choose whether or not spanking is an acceptable form of discipline. If we simply repeat spanking because

134

that's what we learned, then we are operating in a space called "forgetfulness of being."

Martin Heidegger referred to "forgetfulness of being" as that space where you are absent or preoccupied with something other than what actually is happening at any particular moment in your life. For example, a mother driving down the highway who turns around to talk with her child in the back seat and crashes into an oncoming car does so in a state of forgetfulness of being. The priority event in her life was driving the car. Slipping into forgetfulness of being can be deadly and end in a state of "being-no-more." Abusers of alcohol and other drugs refer to their experiences as "trips" and escapes from reality.

A nonfatal example of forgetfulness of being is the student who daydreams while listening to a class lecture covering the next test's material. Daydreaming is a way of escaping what's happening.

In family violence, I believe that most abusing parents and spouses operate in this state of forgetfulness of being. They become absent from responsible human behavior and the nurturing necessary for the survival of the family. Forgetfulness of being can be chemically induced with alcohol and other drugs or emotionally created in reaction to stress and hardship.

Forgetfulness of being is the absence of rational attitudes and responsible behavior. To choose a rational attitude brings an individual into responsible relationship with the present, with what's happening now. As the result of reading this book, you probably won't be able to hit your child again without an awareness of the damaging consequences.

Staying out of the state of forgetfulness of being requires a conscious decision on your part. You will need courage to pay attention to life as it's happening. I think the current "empowerment" movement in the helping professions is really nothing more than learning the power of being encouraged and encouraging.

To be empowered is to be an encouraged and encouraging human being.

To be an encouraging parent or spouse, you will need to identify the old internalized conversations that you learned in childhood and are no longer necessary. These conversations are old friends that you've been depending on for years. Here are a few examples of old messages:

- I have to please people at any cost.
- I have to be funny in order to keep the family from fighting.
- I'm not very good at anything.
- I've tried it before and it didn't work.
- I have to be seductive in order to get what I want.
- I have to give orders so they'll know who's the boss.
- I have to spank my kids or they won't mind.
- I can't.
- I'll try.

Old conversations can sabotage anything you attempt before you even get started. A Peanuts cartoon illustrates the point of the past sabotaging the present. Lucy stands in center field, as usual, waiting for an easy fly ball. She steadies herself by thinking, This is easy.

Then the old conversations begin: I've never caught it before! I'm no good at this. Why did it have to come my way in the first place? I can't do this. The ball drops to the ground beside her. Linus is screaming and demanding an explanation.

"I guess the past just got in my eyes!" she responds.

Old conversations can set an attitude that expects failure. New conversations can invite action and success. They represent who we are becoming at the moment they're thought or spoken.

Examples of new conversations are:

- I don't have to please people. I am pleasing as I am.
- I don't have to be a clown when I'm feeling down or frightened.
- I am good enough.
- I know that I am enough and I'll be okay.
- I will encourage my children.
- I can choose my attitudes.
- I can.
- I will do it.

To be empowered, you must be willing to talk the language of becoming an encourager. Put courage into your thoughts and words. If you feel discouraged, that's where your work begins. You will need to change the limits of your thinking. Go outside those former limits.

Stop using words that hurt!
Start using words that help!

Forgive yourself and your parents and choose an attitude of encouragement so that you can get on with your life. It is important to understand that forgiveness does not condone the crime committed or imply acceptance of the circumstances. It is an act of releasing the self from destructive anger, revenge, and hatred.

We don't really have the future or the past. The past is gone and does not exist, except in memories. The future exists only as a possibility. Don Juan, in teaching Carlos Castaneda, said:

> **At any moment that you find yourself hesitating, or if at any moment you find yourself putting off until tomorrow trying some new piece of behavior that you could do today, or doing something you've done before, then all you need to do is glance over your left shoulder and there will be a fleeting shadow. That shadow represents your death, and at any moment it might step forward, place its hand on your shoulder and take you. So that the act that you are presently engaged in might be your very last act and therefore fully representative of you.[15]**

It is, therefore, indulgent to hesitate. When you hesitate, you are acting as though you have all the time in the world to change, and you do not! This matter of ending family violence can't wait for the future.

A favorite existential question I ask clients is, "If you were to die in the next five minutes, would you want to be doing what you are doing?" If the answer is no, and it usually is, change is necessary and immediately urgent. Every moment, every day becomes a priority to be made meaningful and enjoyable. I encourage parents to treat every interaction with their children as their last.

This existential thinking is not meant to be fatalistic. It is meant to bring a new meaning to life so that parent-child relationships and families will not miss one another like ships passing in the night.

This book is about bringing a new way of thinking and being into your life in order to stop any family violence. I encourage you to make a new beginning. Family violence can and must be stopped. The stand that I invite you to take in stopping family violence includes the following basic principles:

1. Abuse and violence are not acceptable in the home or anywhere in society. People are not for hitting. Not now, not then, not ever. There is no moral or legal justification for violence.

   The National Council on Child Abuse and Neglect reports that society's acceptance of physical punishment of children is a factor leading to child abuse in our society. A national campaign is needed that matches the intensity of the antidrug war in teaching the maxim "Just Say No" to abuse and violence. The home must be a safe environment.

2. Families are the foundation of our society. However the family goes, so goes society. The home is a miniature environment of democracy, freedom, and peace. If it's autocratic, punitive, and violent, society will become autocratic, punitive, and violent. Our culture shifts and changes as our children move out of the home and into the management of the world. The state of the nation, therefore, is a mirror of how our families are doing. As Erich Fromm writes, "The most important influence on a child is the character of [his or her] parents, rather than this or that single event."[16]

3. Corporal punishment in our homes and public school systems needs to be outlawed. Our homes and our schools must prioritize the preparation of citizens for society. Twenty-two states are leading the way in abolishing corporal punishment in the school system. But we're not among the thirty-one civilized nations that have abolished the practice. Those thirty-one nations are: Poland (1783), Holland (1820), Italy (1860), Belgium (1867), Austria (1870), France (1881), Finland (1890), Russia Union (1917), Turkey (1923), Norway (1936), Rumania (1948), Portugal (1950), Sweden (1958), Denmark (1967), Spain (1967), Germany (1970), Switzerland (1970), United Kingdom (1986), Ireland (1987), and, most recently, China, Cyprus, Ecuador, Greece, Iceland, Israel, Ithar, Japan, Jordan, Luxembourg, Matar, Netherlands, New Zealand, and Philippines. We have a long way to go. If corporal punishment is still tolerated in your state or school

district, you can write your senators and representatives to help us join these countries in taking a stand for our children.

4. Our commitment to stopping family violence is centered on education and raising individual and public consciousness. Support parent education workshops and the National Council on Child Abuse and Neglect in the distribution of new information and programs for stopping family violence. Be active in parent-teacher organizations and work together on stopping family violence and corporal punishment in the school system.

5. Individual, marriage, family, and group therapy in cooperation with social services are a priority in providing services for the abused. Community support of shelters for battered spouses, children, and the elderly needs to be a number-one priority when you vote. Family therapists in private practice and counseling agencies, communities of faith, and departments of family and children services provide a milieu (holistic) team approach to healing and changing attitudes about family violence.

6. When victims or perpetrators refuse to seek help, outside intervention must stop the abuse. Court-ordered therapy can be just as effective as voluntary therapy. The priority is to stop the abuse, with or without the consent of the perpetrators. Perpetrators often are relieved to be "found out" and respond well to therapeutic intervention. The home is a private place as long as it is healthy and safe. When it becomes unhealthy and dangerous, it loses its freedom to be autonomous. There are no boundaries once family violence occurs.

7. Stopping family violence in this decade is a priority. Child abuse and neglect have our president's attention. But family violence must become the priority of Congress, states and counties, municipalities and communities, families and individuals. Our government is of the people, by the people, and for the people. Family violence can be stopped if we, the people, decide so! Stopping family violence is not something that you or I can do alone. We must all do this together. We must believe that this is possible, and we must believe in one another!

One evening, a crowd gathered at the Concert Hall in Chicago. They were angry because the great maestro was ill with laryngitis. They would not hear the beautiful voice of the singer they had come to hear.

As the curtain rose, the understudy stepped forward and sang beautifully. He performed flawlessly throughout the entire first act. The act came to a close, and although he had sung and acted the role as well as the star, there was no applause. The unforgiving audience was silent. They wanted their hero.

Finally, from one of the box seats off to the right, came the sound of one small pair of hands applauding. All eyes turned to see the six-year-old son of the understudy standing, clapping vigorously. He shouted, "Beautiful, Daddy! Beautiful! I believe in you!"

And the whole audience erupted with applause.

In taking a stand for stopping violence, let's applaud one another and affirm our belief, so that the whole audience of our nation will join us.

In order to change, we will need coaching. A person who teaches himself or herself to play golf may do okay for a while but frequently develops unskilled golf habits. The best way to correct those limiting habits is by taking lessons from a skilled instructor. Coaching is a sharing of new information that works, if practiced. If you're not willing to change old habits, you can't be coached. The most efficient way that coaching works is when the player involved has something at stake. If you're playing baseball and I'm coaching football, you won't learn much.

The late, great Bear Bryant was coaching Alabama several years ago. With less than a minute to play in the fourth quarter, Alabama was ahead by two points. Coach Bryant knew he had a young, inexperienced quarterback, so he called time-out to have a talk with the lad. He told the jubilant young man to take the snap and fall on the ball and let the clock run out. Whatever he did, he was not to throw the ball.

Play resumed and the excited quarterback lined up and saw that the other team was not expecting a pass. He decided to call an audible at the line of scrimmage. He reasoned that he could burn the other team for a quick six. As you might expect, the fastest man on the other team intercepted and streaked down the sidelines toward a winning touchdown. No one on Alabama's team could catch him—except the quarterback. He ran that fellow down at the three-yard line and tackled him just as the gun went off, and the game was over. Alabama won.

At midfield, the other team's coach said to Bear, "I don't understand it. The slowest man on your team outran the fastest man on my team. How did he do it?"

Bear Bryant is reported not to have cracked even a smile in his reply. "It's very simple," he said. "Your man was running for a touchdown. My man, he was running for his [bleeping] life!"[17]

The stakes are high in stopping family violence: human life and dignity. Whether or not you are a victim or perpetrator of abuse does not matter; these stakes are high enough to command everyone's attention.

A new era is upon us. The world is responding to the need for increased collaboration and cooperation. Autocracies are crumbling and being replaced with solidarity and democratic cooperation. This shift is based on the fundamental principle that power is a vital strength that expands when shared and that empowerment is the action of responsibility in freedom of choice and an expression of encouragement.

A Working Understanding of Empowerment

Empowerment is taking responsibility for one's attitude. Alfred Adler taught that the one basic freedom we have is the freedom to choose our attitude at any time and under any circumstance. An example of this is in Martin Luther's statement, "And if I were told that the world would be destroyed tomorrow, I would plant a tree."

We are empowered when we are choosing our attitudes and claiming responsibility for our choices. To be empowered means to be responsible for every decision that I make, to know that I am not a victim of circumstances but that I most often participate in creating the circumstances of my experiences. To be empowered does not release me from the consequences of my actions. It places me in direct relatedness to the results of my choices. My actions become expressions of my freedom of choice.

Empowerment is more simple than it sounds and as powerful as it sounds! It is saying what you mean, meaning what you say, and following through.

Empowerment is paying attention to life, not missing the moment. Yesterday is gone and tomorrow may not get here. Time becomes a priority when we understand that for millions of years we did not exist and for millions of years we won't exist; we have only fifty to a hundred years at most. This little speck of matter in a microscopic time zone is all we have. This perspective helps us begin to choose what's important. Your choices and decisions become more focused and empowered when you develop priorities. Today is the tomorrow you worried about yesterday. Was it worth it?!

Empowerment is living your words. You are your words, and you become your words. Whatever the community is saying about you, whether you like it or not, you have influenced and generated. Empowerment is choosing the conversations you want "out there" about who you are.

The future is a combination of today's and yesterday's messages. The future, if based more on yesterday's conversations than on those of today, will be as yesterday. The best predictor of future behavior is past performance. Therefore, the future depends on the careful selection of memories that we move forward from the past to today and the new memories that we're creating today.

By carefully selecting our memories, we design our future and live it. This enhancement of the future draws us forward toward the experience we are creating. It has been said that "without a vision do people perish." Vision is a "seeing through" hope for tomorrow. Such vision requires working on the edge of our being, not impeded by consciousness. Consciousness is a necessary beginning for change, yet recedes with true progress. If this seems confusing, examine the following example.

It takes conscious mental rehearsal—practice—to learn how to play a guitar. Each note is strummed slowly and methodically, then faster and faster. Finally the fingers and hands are dancing over the strings and frets while playing a song. Consciousness has moved out of the way.

The same is true of our language. We began as infants with mental rehearsals of sounds and syllables. Today, as adults, we do not consciously think about each word. We speak words unconsciously, just as the musician's fingers play notes. The mind, mouth, and other language-producing organs follow the tracks practiced. Thus, change occurs when we stop a behavior, deal with the feelings created by the loss, and begin designing new tracks, new grooves for our unconsciousness.

Only when we stop trying to control lives do we let our present possibilities unfold. As long as we're trying to control life with consciousness—that is, slow, meticulous, mechanical ordering of our environment—we are not creative. A breakthrough is imminent when we stop controlling and start designing. Controlling life limits possibilities. Designing life creates many possibilities. A controlled life is boring. It is the essence of codependency. A designed life is exciting. It brings with it new ways of being and doing things!

Empowerment is standing for one another in a cooperative way. I. F. Nye, Ph.D., past president of the National Council on Family Relations, wrote in *Choice, Exchange, and the Family* that, in standing for one another, we must achieve what is known in the exchange theory as maximum joint profit (MJP). The goal of social intercourse is maximum joint profit, where both parties in an exchange feel satisfied with what is given and received.

Social life, says I. F. Nye, requires reciprocity. A norm of reciprocity assumes that you treat people who have been kind to you with kindness, with fair exchanges. If you exhibit anger, you receive anger. If you encourage, you will be encouraged. If you cooperate, people will cooperate with you. Humans realize that their choices affect the rewards and costs of other members of the groups to which they belong. Empowerment is making choices that result in maximum joint profit and the norm of reciprocity.

Another maxim of the exchange theory is that "those who receive what they feel they deserve feel satisfied. Those who receive less feel anger. Those who receive more feel guilt." Whether you're working on your career, private life, marriage, or partnership, you need a sufficient network of people standing for you.[18]

In Alfred Adler's theory of personality development, he began with the concept that the human psyche was powerfully affected by organ inferiority. Through the years, man changed in a process that moved through the stages given below and ended in his social interest as being indicative of good mental health.

Organ Inferiority

Psychological Inferiority

Aggression/Will to Power

Striving for Superiority

Striving to Belong

Striving to Contribute

Social Interest

Mental health is equivalent to one's social interest! Empowerment is being engaged in community—with a sense of belonging, contribution, and concerned actions for the well-being of the community. As long as we are consumed with inferiority complexes, aggressive behaviors, power addictions, and perfectionism, we are more concerned about what we are going to get out of life. Frankly, the world does not care what you get. It cares what you contribute. To be empowered is to move to the process of becoming a contributor, to being socially involved where you are needed.

The more aware we are of the interconnectedness of all people, the healthier we are. When we realize, for instance, that the air we breathe has been inside the lungs of the Chinese, Russian, and Central American people, we begin to value life from a new perspective of appreciation and relatedness.

The world needing you to be empowered is more powerful than your needing to be empowered.

The task of empowerment is to help design your world so that it needs you to be empowered. Ask the world what it needs from you. What is the world calling you to be? You must stay within your possibilities. A mechanic who feels that the world is calling him to be a research scientist will not be empowered if he takes on this calling without adequate preparation. We need to test our aspirations with the reality of who we are. Contributing is good mental health. It's that simple.

One of the ways to know that you're empowered is when you're empowering others. You empower others by standing for them and contributing to their lives.

By now you probably have taken several steps toward stopping family violence. If you need further assistance in stopping family violence in your own life, seek professional help.

How to Seek Professional Help

Seek help with licensed marriage and family therapists, pastoral counselors, psychologists, and other professional counselors who have been trained in the treatment of family violence. If possible, ask for a referral from someone who has had a good experience with a particular therapist. Meet with the counselor. If you feel that the therapist has a genuine interest in you and is well qualified in the area of your concern, your work can begin. If not, keep interviewing therapists until you find the one you want.

Don't be afraid to ask questions about credentials, training, and opinions about your problem—for example, ask how they feel about physical discipline. Ask about treatment plans and costs. (But remember, inexpensive therapy that isn't good is a bad deal. You often get what you pay for.)

If money is an issue, you can still get help. Clinical members of the American Association of Marriage and Family Therapists (AAMFT) are expected to donate a percentage of their therapy schedule per year to indigent families and individuals. United Way agencies can help, and community mental health centers—though often overloaded and understaffed—can provide sliding-fee services. Don't give up if you're broke. *Help is out there.* Finding a helping professional who works well with you is an important part of your recovery.

Therapy can be very expensive. If you have a low income or are financially stressed, you can find sliding-fee-scale counseling if you're willing to look for it. Many adjustable-rate counseling settings provide services via clinical students in supervision. This can be some of the best therapy available, since AAMFT supervisors keep abreast of the most current and effective treatment modalities.

Third-party coverage and other programs may cover some of the expense. Many medical insurance companies do not recognize family violence as a covered expense. They hold to the old "medical" model that pays only psychiatrists and licensed psychologists. Unfortunately, not all psychiatrists and psychologists are trained in treating family violence. Community mental health centers, the departments of family and children services, family counseling agencies, and private practitioners are all listed in the Yellow Pages.

Be cautious with any corporate, monopoly-type institution whose first question to you on the phone or in person is, "do you have insurance?" Such institutions can cost up to $20,000 for one month's inpatient care. They often provide community service programs as a guise for building their megabucks empire and are more profit motivated than services inspired.

Help is out there. But *you have to make the call!*

My eight-year-old daughter brought home a statement from the United Nations that she is learning in school. It's an appropriate ending to this conversation on changing the way we think.

I am a member of the world family. I am related to those who stand next to me by the air we breathe, by the light we share and the hope we have for a better world.

I have a responsibility to give, to receive, to be open, to be tolerant and free. I have inherited this world from those who have lived here before. I occupy space and time for a few years. I hold this world in trust for those who will follow.

My life, with others, can fashion this world toward peace, rather than strife, hope, rather than despair, freedom, rather than slavery.

I, with those about me, can make the brotherhood of man a living thing. I pledge my willing spirit to this thought.

We will do this together.

We *can* stop family violence. We will do this together, and our homes will be safe.

NOTES

1. C. Whitaker, *From Psyche to System: The Evolving Therapy of Carl Whitaker* (New York: Guilford Press, 1982), p. 366.

2. W. Durant, *The Pleasures of Philosophy: An Attempt at a Consistent Philosophy of Life* (New York: Simon and Schuster, 1929), p. 100.

3. "Nasrudin," *Sermon Notes*, 1989.

4. C. G. Jung, *The Development of Personality* (New York: Pantheon Books, 1954), p. 190.

5. Ibid., p. 191.

6. Ibid., p. 194.

7. Durant, p. 150.

8. K. Gibran, *The Prophet* (New York: Alfred A. Knopf, 1923), p. 16.

9. J. Kavanaugh, *A Fable* (New York: Dutton, 1980), pp. 61-62.

10. National PTA (700 North Rush Street, Chicago, IL 60611-2571).

11. My thanks to Tim Evans, Ph.D., professor of Adlerian Family Therapy at the University of Georgia, and the gift of his book *The Art of Encouragement* (Athens: University of Georgia Center for Continuing Education, 1989), and to Dr. John Dagley, professor of Adlerian Family Therapy at the University of Georgia. This section of chapter 4 has been greatly influenced by their presentation of Adlerian principles of encouragement and the six goals of misbehavior.

12. R. Dreikurs, *Children: The Challenge* (New York: Hawthorn Books, 1964).

13. Tim Evans, classroom lecture, Counseling Department, University of Georgia, 1989.

14. A more detailed presentation of family council meetings is available through Dr. Michael Popkin, Active Parenting, 810 Franklin Ct., Marietta, GA 30067.

15. C. Castaneda, *The Eagle's Gift* (New York: Simon and Schuster, 1981).

16. E. Fromm, *The Anatomy of Human Destructiveness* (New York: Holt, Rinehart and Winston, 1973), p. 371.

17. *Pulpit Helps* (Chattanooga, 1987).

18. I. F. Nye, *Choice, Exchange, and the Family: Contemporary Theories about the Family* (New York: Free Press, 1979).

ABOUT THE AUTHOR

Jerry Brinegar, Ph.D. is a nationally recognized therapist, workshop leader, and writer. He is author of *Breaking Free from Violence* (1986), a training manual for helping professionals working with domestic violence. He is an approved supervisor in the American Association of Marriage and Family Therapists and a Certified Family Life Educator in the National Council on Family Relations. Licensed as a marriage and family therapist in Georgia and North Carolina, Dr. Brinegar, a Vietnam veteran and former Atlanta police officer, has seventeen years of experience in private practice working with family violence. He has been recognized as one of the three top experts in police stress and domestic crisis intervention in the nation. He is the director of New Beginnings Marriage and Family Therapy in Athens, Georgia.

APPENDIX A

National Organizations that Can Help

American Humane Association
63 Inverness Drive East
Englewood, CO 80112-5117
303-792-9900

American Professional Society on the Abuse of Children
P.O. Box 34028
Los Angeles, CA 90034-0028
213-836-2471

C. Henry Kempe Center
1205 Oneida Street
Denver, CO 80220
303-321-3963

Center for the Prevention of Sexual and Domestic Violence
An Interreligious Educational Ministry
1914 North Thirty-fourth Street, Suite 105
Seattle, WA 98103-9058
206-634-1903

Child Help National Child Abuse Hotline
P.O. Box 630
Hollywood, CA 90028
1-800-422-4453

Child Protection Program, Incorporated
7441 Marvin D. Love Freeway, Suite 200
Dallas, TX 75237
214-709-0300

Family Violence and Sexual Assault Institute
1310 Clinic Drive
Tyler, TX 75701
903-595-6600

Incest Survivors Resource Network International
P.O. Box 7375
Las Cruces, NM 88006-7375
505-521-4260

National Association for Children of Alcoholics
11426 Rockville Pike, Suite 100
Rockville, MD 20852
301-468-0985

National Center on Child Abuse and Neglect
U.S. Department of Health and Human Services
P.O. Box 1182
Washington, D.C. 20013
202-245-0586

National Child Abuse Hotline
1-800-422-4453
1-800-4 A CHILD

National Committee for the Prevention of Child Abuse
320 South Michigan Avenue, #950
Chicago, IL 60604
312-633-3520

National Council on Child Abuse and Family Violence
1155 Connecticut Avenue NW
Washington, D.C. 20036
202-429-6695
800-222-2000

National Domestic Violence Hotline
1-800-333-7233
1-800-873-6363—Hearing Impaired

National Organization for Victim Assistance
1757 Park Road NW
Washington, D.C. 20010
202-232-6682
1-800-TRY-NOVA (879-6682)

National Research Center
American Association for Protecting Children
Division of American Humane Association
63 Inverness Drive East
Englewood, CO 80112-5117
1-800-227-5242

National Victim Center
309 West Seventh Street, Suite 705
Fort Worth, TX 76102
817-877-3355

Parents against Child Abuse
Department P
P.O. Box 1262
Temecula, CA 92390

Parents Anonymous
1-800-421-0353

Public Awareness about Child Care
Department P
P.O. Box 545, Station 12
930 South Monaco
Denver, CO 80224-1665

Sexual Assault Center
Harborview Medical Center
325 Ninth Avenue, 2A-07
Seattle, WA 98104
206-223-3047

Survivors of Incest Anonymous
P.O. Box 21817
Baltimore, MD 21222
301-282-3400

Vanished Children's Alliance
1407 Parkmoor Avenue, Suite 200
San Jose, CA 95126
1-800-VANISHED

HELP FOR HELPING PROFESSIONALS

You will find my first book, *Breaking Free from Violence*, quite helpful. It is a training manual for law enforcement officers and other helping professionals who deal directly with domestic violence and crisis situations. It includes domestic crisis intervention, stress management techniques, and skills that will maximize your safety. You can order *Breaking Free from Violence* by calling 404-548-1668. I invite you to join me in my stand against family violence. Let's network! Describe your interests and programs by writing to: New Beginnings Marriage and Family Therapy, Inc., 555 Research Drive, Suite D-2, Athens, GA 30605, 404-548-1668.

APPENDIX B

The Twelve Steps of Alcoholics Anonymous

1. We admitted we were powerless over alcohol—that our lives had become unmanageable.

2. Came to believe that a Power greater than ourselves could restore us to sanity.

3. Made a decision to turn our will and our lives over to the care of God, as we understood Him.

4. Made a searching and fearless moral inventory of ourselves.

5. Admitted to God, to ourselves, and to another human being the exact nature of our wrongs.

6. Were entirely ready to have God remove all these defects of character.

7. Humbly asked Him to remove our shortcomings.

8. Made a list of all persons we had harmed, and became willing to make amends to them all.

9. Made direct amends to such people wherever possible, except when to do so would injure them or others.

10. Continued to take personal inventory and when we were wrong, promptly admitted it.

11. Sought through prayer and meditation to improve our conscious contact with God, as we understood Him, praying only for knowledge of His will for us and the power to carry that out.

12. Having had a spiritual awakening as the result of these steps, we tried to carry this message to alcoholics, and to practice these principles in all our affairs.

BIBLIOGRAPHY

Abel, G. G., J. V. Becker, and L. J. Skinner. *Behavioral Approaches to Treatment of the Violent Sex Offender.* DHHS publication no. ADM 85-1425, Washington, D.C., 1985.

Adler, A. *The Education of Children.* London: Allen and Unwin, 1957.

———. *Social Interest: A Challenge to Mankind.* New York: Putnam, 1939.

Armstrong, L. *Kiss Daddy Goodnight.* New York: Pocket Books, 1979.

Back, S. "Ethical Issues in Family Violence Research." Paper presented at the Second National Conference for Family Violence Researchers, Durham, New Hampshire, 1983.

Bass, E., and L. Davis, *The Courage to Heal.* New York: Harper and Row, 1988.

Becker, J., L. J. Skinner, G. G. Abel, and E. C. Treacy. "Incidence and Types of Sexual Dysfunctions in Rape and Incest Victims." *Journal of Sex and Marital Therapy,* 8 (1982): 65-74.

Blackman, N., and D. Hellman. "Enuresis, Firesetting, and Cruelty to Animals: A Triad Predictive of Adult Crime." *American Journal of Psychiatry* 122 (1966): 1431-35.

Bleiszner, R., and J. M. Alley. "Family Care-Giving for the Elderly: An Overview of Resources." *Family Relations, Journal of Applied Family and Child Studies* 39 (1990): 1.

Blumberg, M. "When Parents Hit Out." *Twentieth Century* 173 (1965): 39-44.

Boatman, E., E. L. Borkan, and D. H. Schetky. "Treatment of Child Victims of Incest." *American Journal of Family Therapy* 9 (1981): 42-51.

Bowker, L. *Beating Wife Beating.* Lexington, Mass.: Lexington Books, 1983.

Brinegar, J. L. *Breaking Free from Violence.* New York: Gardner Press, 1986.

———. *Empowerment I, Workshop Guide.* Athens, Ga.: New Beginnings Marriage and Family Therapy, 1990.

Browne, A., and D. Finkelhor. "Impact of Child Sexual Abuse: A Review of the Research." *Psychological Bulletin* 99, no. 1 (1986): 66-77.

Carper, J. J. *Incest.* Pediatric Clinics of North America, 1976.

Carter, J. *The Maltreated Child.* London: Priority Press, 1974.

Castaneda, C. *The Eagle's Gift*. New York: Simon and Schuster, 1981.

Cobbe, F. P. "Wife Torture in England." *Contemporary Review*, 1878, pp. 32, 55-87.

Cochran, P., and M. Young. *The Violent Mind*. Pleasantville, N.Y.: Human Relations Media (filmstrip booklet), 1982.

Cooper, W. *Flagellation and the Flagellants: A History of the Rod in All Ages and Countries*. London: Hotten, 1873.

Day, R., ed. *Plain Talk about Wife Abuse*. National Institute of Mental Health, Division of Scientific and Public Information. DHHS publication no. ADM 83-1265, 1983.

Deschner, J. P. *The Hitting Habit: Anger Control for Battering Couples*. New York: Free Press, 1984.

Dreikurs, R. *Adult-Child Relations*. Alfred Adler Institute, 1967.

———. *Children: The Challenge*. New York: Hawthorn Books, 1964.

———. *Discipline without Tears*. New York: Dutton, 1972.

———. *Logical Consequences: A New Approach to Discipline*. New York: Dutton, 1968.

Durant, W. *The Pleasures of Philosophy: An Attempt at a Consistent Philosophy of Life*. New York: Simon and Shuster, 1929.

Eisikovits and Edleson. "Interviewing with Men Who Batter: A Critical Review of the Literature." *Social Service Review*, September 1989, 384-414.

Evans, Tim, Ph.D. *The Art of Encouragement*. Athens: University of Georgia Department of Continuing Education, 1989.

Finkelhor, D. *A Sourcebook on Child Sexual Abuse*. Newbury Park, Calif.: Sage Publications, 1986.

Finkelhor, D., and L. Baron. "Risk Factors for Child Sexual Abuse." *Journal of Interpersonal Violence* 1 (1986): 43-71.

Finkelhor, D., G. T. Hotaling, and K. Yllo. *Stopping Family Violence: Research Priorities for the Coming Decade*. Newbury Park, Calif.: Sage Publications, 1988.

Forward, S. *Toxic Parents*. New York: Bantam Books, 1989.

Forward, S., and C. Buck. *Betrayal of Innocence: Incest and Its Devastation*. New York: Penguin Books, 1979.

Fromm, E. *The Anatomy of Human Destructiveness*. New York: Holt, Rinehart and Winston, 1990.

Galdston, R. "Preventing the Abuse of Little Children: The Parents' Center Project for the Study and Prevention of Child Abuse." *American Journal of Orthopsychiatry* 45 (1975): 372·81.

Gelles, R. J. *The Violent Home: A Study of Physical Aggression between Husbands and Wives*. Newbury Park, Calif.: Sage Publications, 1974.

Gelles, R. J., and C. C. Pedrick. *Intimate Violence in Families*. Beverly Hills, Calif.: Sage Publications, 1985.

Gibran, K. *The Prophet*. New York: Alfred A. Knopf, 1923.

Gil, D. G. *Violence against Children: Physical Abuse in the United States*. Cambridge, Mass.: Harvard University Press, 1970.

Gil, E. *Treatment of Adult Survivors of Childhood Abuse*. Walnut Creek, Calif.: Launch Press, 1988.

Gray, J. D., et al. "Prediction and Prevention of Child Abuse and Neglect." *Child Abuse and Neglect* 1 (1977): 45·68.

Halleck, S. L. "The Physician's Role in Management of Victims of Sex Offenders." *Journal of the American Medical Association* 180 (1962): 273·78.

Hansen, J. C. *Clinical Approaches to Family Violence*. Rockville, Md.: Aspen Publications, 1982.

Heidegger, M. *Being and Time*. New York: Harper and Row, 1962.

Helfer, R., and C. Kempe. *The Battered Child*. Chicago: University of Chicago Press, 1974.

Herrenkohl, E., R. Herrenkohl, and L. Roedter. *Perspectives on the Intergenerational Transmission of Abuse, the Dark Side of Families: Current Family Violence Research*. Newbury Park, Calif.: Sage Publications, 1983.

Highlights of Official Child Neglect and Abuse Report 1984. Denver: American Humane Association. American Association for Protecting Children, 1986.

Hoffman, B. *No One Is to Blame*. Palo Alto, Calif.: Science and Behavior Books, 1979.

Jung, C. G. *The Development of Personality*. New York: Pantheon Books, 1954.

Justice, B., and R. Justice. *The Broken Taboo: Sex in the Family*. New York: Human Science Press, 1979.

Kavanaugh, J. *A Fable*. New York: Dutton, 1980.

Kempe, C., F. Silverman, and B. Steele. "The Battered Child Syndrome." *Journal of the American Medical Association* 181 (1962): 1.

Krishnamurti, J. *Beyond Violence.* New York: Krishnamurti Foundation Trust, 1973.

Kuczen, B. *Childhood Stress.* New York: Delacorte, 1982.

Light, R. J. "Abused and Neglected Children in America: A Study of Alternative Policies." *Harvard Educational Review* 43 (November 1974): 556-98.

Lincoln, A. J., and M. A. Straus. *Crime and the Family.* Springfield, Ill.: Charles C. Thomas, 1985.

Lorenz, K. *On Aggression.* New York: Harcourt, Brace and World, 1963.

Madden, D. J. "Psychotherapy with Violent Patients." *Psychiatric Annals* 12 (1982): 517-21.

Martin, J. P., ed. *Violence and the Family.* New York: John Wiley and Sons, 1978.

May, R. *Power and Innocence: A Search for the Sources of Violence.* New York: W. W. Norton, 1972.

McCord, J. "A Forty-Year Perspective on Effects of Child Abuse and Neglect." *Child Abuse and Neglect* 7 (1983): 265-70.

Murstein, B. I. "Stimulus-Value-Role: A Theory of Marital Choice." *Journal of Marriage and Family Therapy* 32 (1970).

Nye, I. F. *Choice, Exchange, and the Family: Contemporary Theories about the Family.* New York: Free Press, 1979.

Parnas, R. L. "The Police Response to Domestic Disturbance." *Wisconsin Law Review* 914 (Fall 1967): 914-60.

Perry, M. J. "Problem Gains Attention." *In Focus: Elder Abuse*, November 1985, ASA Connection.

Pillemer, K., and D. Finkelhor. "The Prevalence of Elder Abuse: A Random Sample Survey." *Gerontologist* 28 (1988): 51-57.

Popkin, M. *Leader's Guide, Active Parenting.* New York: Harper and Row, 1987.

Radecki, T. "War Games." *National Council on TV Violence News*, 10 (November 1989-January 1990): 3.

Roy, M. *The Abusive Partner.* New York: Van Nostrand Reinhold, 1982.

Schaef, A. W. "We're a Nation of Addicts." *New Age Journal*, March-April 1987.

Schrieber, F. R. *Sybil.* New York: Warner Books, 1973.

Snell, J. E., R. J. Rosenwald, and A. Robey. "The Wifebeater's Wife: A Study of Family Interaction." *Archives of General Psychiatry* 11 (August 1964): 107-13.

Sonkin, D. J., and M. Durphy. *Learning to Live without Violence*. San Francisco: Family Violence Project, 1981.

Spinetta, J. J., and D. Rigler. "The Child Abusing Parent: A Psychological Review." *Psychological Bulletin* 77 (April 1972): 296-304.

Steinmetz, S. K. *Duty Bound: Elder Abuse and Family Care*. Newbury Park, Calif.: Sage Publications, 1988.

———. *Family Violence, Past, Present, Future*. Newark: University of Delaware, 1971.

Steinmetz, S. K., and M. A. Straus. *Violence in the Family*. New York: Harper and Row, 1974.

Straus, M. A. "A General Systems Approach to the Development of a Theory of Violence between Family Members." *Social Science Information* 12 (June 1973): 105-25.

———. "2001: Preparing Families for the Future." National Council on Family Relations Presidential Report, January 1990.

Straus, M. A., and R. J. Gelles. "Societal Change in Family Violence from 1975 to 1985 as Revealed by Two National Surveys." *Journal of Marriage and Family* 48 (1986): 465-79.

Straus, M. A., R. J. Gelles, and S. K. Steinmetz. *Behind Closed Doors: Violence in the American Family*. Newbury Park, Calif.: Sage Publications, 1980.

Walker, L. *The Battered Woman*. New York: Harper and Row, 1979.

Whitaker, C. *From Psyche to System: The Evolving Therapy of Carl Whitaker*. New York: Guilford Press, 1982.

Wisechild, Louise M. *The Obsidian Mirror: An Adult Healing from Incest*. Seattle: Seal Press, 1988.

Woititz, J. G. *Adult Children of Alcoholics*. Pompano Beach, Fla.: Health Communications, 1983.